FERMENTATION

A Firefly Book

Published by Firefly Books Ltd. 2023
Originally published in French as:
Au coeur de la fermentation
Usages, histoire et recettes
© Flammarion, 2022
Texts © Mathilde Fenestraz and Stéphane Ros
Bread recipes © Marie-Laure Fréchet (pages 102–112)
Photography and styling © Studio Tekhné (cover, pages 49–149, 203)
and Nicolas Villion (cover, pages 157–195)
Illustrations © Sixtine Ros
Production: Julie Hautecourt & Louisa Hanifi

All rights reserved. No part of this publication may be reproduced, stored in a retrieval system, or transmitted in any form or by any means, electronic, mechanical, photocopying, recording or otherwise, without the prior written permission of the Publisher.

First printing

Library of Congress Control Number: 2022945768

Library and Archives Canada Cataloguing in Publication
Title: Fermentation : history, uses and recipes / Mathilde Fenestraz ; preface and a history of fermentation, Stéphane Ros ; photography and styling, Studio Tekhné, Nicolas Villion ; illustrations, Sixtine Ros.
Names: Fenestraz, Mathilde, author.
Description: Includes bibliographical references.
Identifiers: Canadiana 20220423423 | ISBN 9780228104117 (hardcover)
Subjects: LCSH: Fermented foods. | LCSH: Fermentation—History. | LCSH: Fermented beverages. | LCSH: Cooking (Fermented foods)
Classification: LCC TP371.44 .F46 2023 | DDC 641.4/63—dc23

Published in Canada by	Published in the United States by
Firefly Books Ltd.	Firefly Books (U.S.) Inc.
50 Staples Avenue, Unit 1	P.O. Box 1338, Ellicott Station
Richmond Hill, Ontario	Buffalo, New York
L4B 0A7	14205

Editorial Partnerships: Henri Julien & Lucie Baudin
Editorial Project Management: Laetitia Réal-Moretto
Translation: Anne McDowall & Carmella Moreau
Art Direction and Design: David Cosson - Dazibaocom
Copy-editing and Proofreading: Marc Feustel
Production: Christelle Lemonnier & Louisa Hanifi
Colour Separation: IGS-CP

Printed in Slovenia

MATHILDE FENESTRAZ

Preface and A History of Fermentation
STÉPHANE ROS

FERMENTATION
History, Uses and Recipes

Photography and Styling
STUDIO TEKHNE
NICOLAS VILLION
Illustrations
SIXTINE ROS

FIREFLY BOOKS

CONTENTS

Preface 6

A HISTORY OF FERMENTATION 8

GOING BACK TO THE ORIGINS OF FERMENTATION 10
Inert matter becomes living matter 10
A medium for the divinities 14
Well-established traditions 18
Making food easier to digest 20
Preserving and gathering: a constant problem 23
Improvement 24
Health benefits 25

A FERMENT OF CIVILIZATION 28
Common values and culture 28
The Mediterranean triad, or the seeds of a civilization 32
How ferment migrates and travels 35

PASTEURIZATION, DECLINE, AND A NEW BEGINNING 38
The decline 38
Fermentation makes its comeback 42

THE MANY VARIETIES OF FERMENTED FOODS 44

THE ICONIC PRODUCTS 46
Fermented vegetables: plenty of scope for the imagination ... 46
Meat and fish 60
Dairy products 64
Pancakes, crepes, and blinis 70
Hot sauces and ketchup 76

THE CULTURAL IMPORTANCE OF BREAD 80
Bread: a reflection of our cultural diversities 80
The ingredients in bread 90
The fermentation of bread 98
Six easy recipes 102

FERMENTED DRINKS:
ELIXIRS FULL OF ORIGINALITY **116**
Beer **117**
Cider **121**
Wine **124**
Liquors (distilled spirits) **128**
Kombucha **134**
Milk kefir **140**
Water kefir or tibicos **142**
Ginger bug or ginger starter **146**

FERMENTATION AND OUR SENSES **150**

THE THEORY OF FOOD PAIRING
By Agnès Giboreau, Director of Research at the Institut Paul Bocuse **152**

FERMENTED FOOD AND DRINK PAIRINGS
By the Institut Paul Bocuse's experts **156**

Pairing Port with Roquefort by Gaëtan Bouvier **156**
Shu pu'er cha with Tomme de Savoie IGP au Foin by Bernard Ricolleau **160**
Curds with hay by Florent Boivin **164**
Malabar coffee with Camembert by Alain Dauvergne **168**
Miso with tahini by Philippe Bachmann **174**
Sauerkraut with pigeon, juniper, foie gras, and sea urchin by Marc Lahoreau **178**
Chocolate with tarragon by Vincent Durant **184**
Fermented shrimp curry paste with scallops by Florian Pansin **188**
Brioche with framboise beer by Camille Dupuy, Lesaffre **192**

THE FUTURE OF FERMENTATION **196**

PREFACE

To paraphrase Louis Pasteur, who asserted that "fermentation is life without oxygen," you could say that fermentation is life. Omnipresent in our lives and throughout history, the fermentation processes carried out by microorganisms are found at the origin of all human cultures, in food, but also in our bodies, where the billions of microorganisms that make up our immune systems and are responsible for the proper functioning of our organisms have coexisted since the dawn of humanity.

Pioneers of life on Earth, yeast and bacteria inhabit our world and are essential for ensuring our future.

Fermentation has long been the main agent of subsistence. Deriving from the Latin word *fervere*, meaning "to boil," fermentation was the magical way of "cooking" without fire that our ancestors used to preserve food without altering its qualities. Whether in the form of bread, wine, cheese, or cured meats, fermentation is foundational to our civilizations. Today, we are rediscovering the benefits of fermentation, not only for health reasons but also for the taste it imparts. This Terra virtually incognita—omnipresent, yet little known—is central to the original approach adopted by this book on fermentation and fermented foods.

In addition to exploring a history almost as old as humanity, and introducing the many types of fermented products, this book immerses us in a world of stimulating flavors with recipes by the Institut Paul Bocuse.

For Lesaffre, fermentation represents the future, both for its potential in terms of technological innovation and for its ability to feed an ever-increasing global population both healthily and sustainably. By 2050, the world will need to feed nine billion human beings without its natural resources being depleted. This is why Lesaffre, which has been pioneering fermentation worldwide for nearly 170 years, is seeking, in all areas of its business, to better nourish and protect the planet through the inexhaustible resources provided by microorganisms.

We are persuaded that the living micoorganisms in the natural world contain an infinite potential that has yet to be explored. In a spirit of innovation—shared with all our employees and subsidiaries worldwide—we are seeking

to reveal this potential. Working on a global scale, we encourage innovation in all our fields of expertise and areas of our business. Fermentation is a universal phenomenon that affects all civilizations, but one that remains on a human scale, deeply rooted in our environment. It is the specificity of the microbiotic environment that is responsible for the immense diversity of flavors found throughout the world.

With our large international presence, we want to think on a global scale but operate on a local one in order to respect fermentation cultures and highlight their infinite value. Eating bread is one of the simple pleasures of life. It is also something that both situates us in history and projects us into the future. In this book, we want to show the vitally important role that fermentation plays in our lives and how it meets the needs of our time, expanding the palette of flavors, ensuring that our diet contributes to our good health, and promoting sustainable development, all while encouraging us to savor the pleasures of life.

Happy eating and happy reading!

S.R.

A HISTORY OF FERMENTATION

Fermentation is a polarizing issue. Anyone who's fond of a good, smelly cheese or the enticing sound of a crisp baguette, anyone who loves kimchi, miso, kefir, or sauerkraut is all for it. But those who liken fermentation to decay will find it disgusting; for them, fermented food is to be discarded. However, few people are aware of the full range of fermented foods and how pervasive they are in our daily diet—from coffee, bread, and dried sausage to yogurt.

Fermentation underlies all cooking; it is the basis of food preparation in every culture, among all the peoples of the world. Food is naturally the primary cultural legacy bestowed on us by our parents, but the origins of fermentation are lost in the most obscure parts of prehistory. If we take this into account, the important role fermentation plays in building our individual personalities becomes apparent. It's hard to imagine French culture without its bread, wine, butter, and cheese. And what would Japanese culture be without the soy sauce, sake, and miso that is consumed daily?

The world of fermentation that we have inherited is the result of a long, complex history which takes us back to the very foundations of our world.

GOING BACK TO THE ORIGINS OF FERMENTATION

Inert matter becomes living matter

It was only in the nineteenth century that scientists demystified the process of fermentation. But fermentation has been at the center of the human diet for considerably longer. In fact, the history of fermentation is an integral part of the history of humankind. Some forms of the process, like the alcoholic fermentation of fruit, take place without any human intervention. Early on in the development of humankind, the phenomenon must have seemed surprising. It has a magical aspect that is astonishing: when fermentation occurs, an inert food begins to emit gases, react, and even to make noises! Its taste is altered and, if alcoholic fermentation takes place, the alcohol produced triggers a state of well-being. In societies where shamanism is practiced, the resulting psychotropic properties facilitate dialogue with the forces of what they refer to as the "other world."[1] Fermentation, an intermediate state between life and death, is therefore a catalyst of the expressions of humanity's first religious feelings.

Mead, also known as honey wine, is often considered the oldest fermented drink. The simplicity of its recipe is to be found in its Greek name: ὑδρόμελι (Latin name, *hydromeli*), comprising two words, one of which means "water" and the other, "honey." Honey, a nectar produced by bees, is imperishable. Since it never goes bad, it only ferments when it comes into contact with at least two-thirds of its weight of water. For a long time, it was thought that the phenomenon was discovered by hunters who stumbled upon an abandoned bee hive that had been flooded by rain. Whatever the truth of the matter, archaeological traces of mead dating back to the sixth millennium BCE have been found in China. Mead was first and foremost thought to be a gift from the gods, with bees their industrious messengers. Gods of Norse mythology were known to be very partial to mead, which they drank from drinking horns served by the Valkyries.[2] Mead plays a prominent role in Greek mythology: in the myth of Orpheus, it was the drink Zeus gave to Kronos, making him immortal; the Pythia (priestess) of Delphi made her prophesies under the influence of mead to which poisonous plants—such as henbane, which considerably increases the effects of drunkenness—had been added.[3]

It has a magical aspect that is astonishing: when fermentation occurs, an inert food begins to emit gases, react, and even to make noises!

The other major fermented drink found around the world is beer. Like mead, its origins are lost in the distant Neolithic era. The oldest traces of beer, found in the Raqefet Cave in Israel, date back to around 11,000 BCE and predate the Neolithic Revolution—the transition from hunting and gathering to agriculture. Beer, a fermented liquid, also played a role in a spiritual context and was often linked with funerary rites. Such beers, if we can call them that, were actually cocktails combining grains, sweet fruit juices, and honey. In China, Neolithic funerary sites have revealed jars containing the residue of fermented drinks, giving us information on such prehistoric beer cocktails. The starch in the grains that were used was transformed into sugar by malting, a process of sprouting the seeds, then drying and roasting them. Even more surprisingly, malting was also carried out by adding what is known as a beer ferment. Cakes of hot grains were allowed to develop a number of fungi and molds, such as *Aspergillus*. These fungi secrete enzymes that transform starch into sugars, thus enabling the process of alcoholic fermentation to take place.

Such seeding, a symbol of fertility and resurrection, features in many myths. The most famous of these is that of the Egyptian dual goddess Sekhmet/Hathor. Ra, the god of creation, angered by the misconduct of humans, decided to destroy all human life. He sent Sekhmet, the lioness goddess, to annihilate all of humanity. But in her destructive folly, she outdid the wishes of Ra, who then ordered Thoth, the baboon god, to brew a beer with an alcohol content augmented by the addition of date juice to intoxicate the destructive Sekhmet. She swallowed far more than she should have and fell fast asleep. During her sleep, she was transformed into Hathor, the benevolent goddess of love, motherhood, and joy. This myth, taken from the *Book of the Heavenly Cow*, brings together

The Sumerian name for beer was sikaru, meaning "liquid bread," a food the entire society consumed in great quantities.

the magical attributes of the fermented drink, linking it to death, resurrection, and fertility.

The Sumerians, too, attributed magical properties to the fermentation vats in which beer was brewed. Their divine presence manifested itself to transform the most basic, common-or-garden ingredients into a living drink. This explains why a fermentation vat was often found within their temples, a tangible sign of the union between the sovereign of the city-state and Inanna, the goddess of fertility whose marriage to the king was celebrated annually.

The Sumerian name for beer was *sikaru*, meaning "liquid bread," a food the entire society consumed in great quantities. Intoxicating and nutritious, the drink provided an alternative way of consuming cereals. Above all, it was safer than water, which was often of dubious quality and could also transmit disease. In beer, bacterial flora is more easily controlled. Egyptian brewers produced a beer that was very different from the beer we know today. It was called *zythum* (from the Greek word meaning "beer") and was made using "beer loaves" made of flour, malt, and yeast culture that were left to ferment, then cooked and crumbled. Water was poured over the crumbs to activate the fermentation process that would transform the mixture into beer. Wall paintings indicate that this thick beer could be drunk directly from the vessels containing it using a long, angled drinking straw, a usage still in practice in certain African countries.

Early on in Ancient Egypt beer brewing workshops were organized on an almost industrial scale. A large brewery that may from the time of King Narmer, between 3185 and 3125 BCE, and may be the oldest in the world, was discovered in February 2021 by an American-Egyptian team of archaeologists in the Abydos mortuary complex. This facility could brew close to 6,000 gallons (over 22,400 liters) at once, making beer that was sometimes enriched with dates for added sweetness and a higher alcohol content. This discovery illustrates the extent to which beer was considered to be a food, because archaeologists have estimated that the thousands of gallons it produced may have been used as a complement to the salary earned by the 8,800 workers of the royal mortuary complex. This means that each one would have had a daily ration of around 5.25 pints (2.5 liters) of beer.[4]

Although beer production techniques have changed, some fermented drinks, such as Ukrainian and Russian *kvass*, are still made with a technique similar to that used by ancient Egyptian brewers. Although *kvass* is low in alcohol, it is made by fermenting dried rye bread in water, sometimes combined with aromatic herbs, fruit, or honey. It was first mentioned in Slav society when Prince Vladimir was baptized around 988 CE and was the main drink for all social classes during the Middle Ages, a symbol of prosperity for both lords and peasants, who drank it when they worked in the fields.

A medium for the divinities

Primitive beer cocktails sometimes contained psychotropic substances connected with shamanic practices that continue to this day. One example is ayahuasca, consumed by shamans of the Amazon region. The name of this drink in Quechua means "liana of the spirits" or "liana of the dead." It is made of a number of hallucinogenic plants of the Solanaceae family and includes the bark of a liana, *Banisteriopsis caapi*. The mixture is infused and left to ferment in water for at least one night. It is then heated and reduced until it is ready for consumption, when it can produce psychotropic effects. Under the observation of the shaman, believed to have night vision thanks to the beverage, anyone who drinks it will be allowed to glimpse omens as well as the world of the spirits and the dead.[5]

In Mayan culture, the drink made from fermented cacao was used for religious ceremonies and reserved for the exclusive consumption of the priests.

Cacao is a fermented product which, if we go back to the origins of its consumption, had exclusively religious attributes. Found in Mesoamerica in the third millennium BCE, the bean required several fermentations before it was ready to be consumed. An initial fermentation allowed the beans to separate from the pulp, which was used to make a fermented alcoholic beverage. A second fermentation, over three to eight days, raised the temperature of the still-damp bean to 122°F (50°C)—this stage is crucial for the taste of the chocolate. In Mayan culture, the drink made from fermented cacao was used for religious ceremonies and reserved for the exclusive consumption of the priests. They used it as a drink during human sacrifices: the cacao that was diluted in water had chili pepper and annatto added to it to color the drink red and evoke the blood of the sacrifice. The cacao pod symbolized the heart of the sacrifice offered to the gods, as attested by numerous pre-Columbian works of art.[6]

Wine, the drink of the Greek gods, originated in the fifth millennium BCE in a region including present-day Iran, Armenia, and Georgia, where the drink is still fermented and aged in large earthenware jars. After this period, wine spread farther afield, mainly to the Middle East, where Phoenician wine-producing

centers supplied much of the ancient world, Egypt first and foremost. Wine was then adopted throughout the Mediterranean Basin right to the borders of the Alexandrian and Roman empires through part of Asia and Europe. In Greece, Dionysus was the god of wine, which he had created by pouring mead over the dead body of Ampelos to restore him to life as a grapevine. In so doing, he gave humans access to a beverage of immortality, one that was reserved for the gods. To pay homage to Dionysus, the Athenians established festivities called the Dionysia to celebrate wine, its god, and the fertility of both humans and the fields. Drunkenness was exceptionally tolerated during these festivities to pay tribute to the creative force of Dionysus. The libations that ancient religions consecrated to their gods several times daily were more ceremonious and were performed by dropping a few drops of pure wine onto the ground, the altar, or a sacrifice. The libations were a call for divine blessings on the person making them and kept evil away from them.

Fermentation, which gives a new life to harvested grapes, is a symbol of resurrection that widely inspired artists in the Middle Ages.

In line with the culture of the Middle East, the Old Testament places special importance on two fermented foods, bread and wine, in the relationship between God and the Hebrew people. "Wine is as good as life to a man… what life is then to a man that is without wine?" asks Ecclesiasticus.[7] Wine is the symbol of a supernatural force that maintains life. It represents both the promised land and paradise. The enormous bunch of grapes brought back from Canaan that inspired painters such as Poussin signifies the end of the Hebrews' wanderings in the wilderness and the realization of God's promise to them. The grapes of Canaan symbolized the exceptional fertility of the land; the fruit also indicated that they had reached the end of their wanderings. In a similar vein, when God saved Noah from the flood and returned him to dry land, the first thing he did to symbolize his gratitude was to plant a vine.[8]

Like bread, the "foaming wine" from the "blood of the grape"[9] mentioned in Deuteronomy also has a liturgical function. When Abraham returned after his victory over King Kedorlaomer, Melchizedek, a priest and king who prefigures Christ in the New Testament's Epistle to the Hebrews,[10] makes an offering of bread and wine to God.[11] In a continuation of the customs of the Hebrews, the Jewish religion uses wine in rituals such as the kiddush, a blessing pronounced on a cup of wine at the start of the Shabbat, and for Passover, the commemoration of the exodus from Egypt, when a glass of wine is passed from one participant to another at the opening of the ritual seder meal, for each one to take a sip.[12]

Christianity, too, considers fermentation to be a divine miracle. The Catholic sacraments, including the most important, the Eucharist, use two emblematic fermented foodstuffs: bread and wine. In fact, they are the very essence of the mass: a bloodless reproduction of Christ's sacrifice through transubstantiation. Bread and wine become the body and blood of Christ, as he declared to the Apostles during the Last Supper.[13] Fermentation, which gives a new life to harvested grapes, is a symbol of resurrection that widely inspired artists in the Middle Ages, who used the metaphor of the mystic winepress that can be seen on stained glass windows and altarpieces. They illustrate Christ being pressed by the wooden cross, like grapes in a winepress; his blood, the ferment of life, flowing into a vat from which saints drink.[14]

According to the Evangelists, Christ's public life began with the miracle of the Wedding at Cana, where on the third day, according to the Gospel of John,[15] water was changed into wine—a mystic image of the Resurrection through fermentation, which transforms an inert substance into one filled with life. In the Gospels, Jesus multiplied bread, the staff of life, on two occasions so that people could receive His spiritual nourishment—His Word. Jesus himself compared the Kingdom of Heaven to the leaven which ferments and gives life to the dough that represents the world.[16]

When Jesus neared death, a fermented food once again came into play: he drank *posca* from a sponge that a Roman soldier named Stephaton, according to medieval tradition, held out to him at the end of a staff. This posca, traditionally considered to be vinegar (a liquid that has a second life after wine is fermented through acetic fermentation) was in reality a drink consumed by Roman legionaries: poor-quality wine that rapidly turned to vinegar and which, when diluted with water, was appreciated as a thirst-quencher and antiseptic.[17]

Well established traditions

Many of our culinary traditions, not to mention colloquial expressions, arise from the symbiosis between belief and fermentation. In many Christian countries, a risen, yeasted bread is eaten at Easter to allude to the Resurrection, like the pilgrims to Emmaus who recognized the risen Christ by the manner in which he broke the bread. Examples are the Spanish *mona de Pascua* and the *mouna* of North Africa.[18] The former comes from the region of Valencia. It is a sweet yeasted bread—a brioche—made of flour, milk, eggs, and yeast. Preparation for baking begins on the Saturday of Holy Week, when Christ had already died. It rises overnight, an allegory of Christ resuscitated, rising from the tomb. The version made in Alicante is shaped like a crown and is bedecked with an egg in the center, yet another metaphor for new life. This tradition is found throughout Europe: from Italy, where the brioche is shaped like a dove, to Alsace and the German-speaking countries, where bakers make a small brioche shaped like an Easter lamb called the *lamala*.
The custom of christening ships shows how an ancient tradition has persisted through the ages. Greek sailors would pour the blood of the animals they sacrificed to the gods of the sea over their boats. Naturally wine became the symbol of the blood and eventually replaced it. In the nineteenth century, wine was replaced by champagne, a more costly sacrifice. When the bottle broke, the champagne foamed over the hull, presaging a long and happy life for the ship. The custom took on new relevance when, early in the twentieth century, many superstitious sailors accused the White Star Line, which did not christen its liners, to have caused the sinking of the Titanic through negligence. Instead of a bottle of champagne, it was the tip of an iceberg that broke on its hull.

The ritualization of both the preparation and consumption of fermented foods can be explained by the fact that fermentation is a complicated process that has been perfected empirically over thousands of years of practice; there is no room for improvisation or else the "magic" might not work. Every winemaker, every baker needs to go through precise, codified actions to achieve the desired result. Following in the steps of countless predecessors with the aim of reproducing a unique product that testifies to centuries of know-how is

tantamount to entering a school of humility. The Japanese tea ceremony is probably the most extreme example of how the consumption of a fermented drink can be ritualized. It was brought over from China, where it originated. There, tea leaves were fermented and then compressed into cakes or bricks to be dried. To prepare the drink, water was added and sometimes, milk and salt too. During the twelfth century, under the Southern Song dynasty, a finely ground green powder was emulsified with hot water to serve as a drink. This custom disappeared in China but was brought to medieval Japan where the custom continues to this very day. This green tea, matcha, is closely associated with Zen Buddhism, whose codes and simplicity are part and parcel of the tea ceremony. Its energizing properties helped Buddhist monks to meditate late into the night. The *chanoyu*, the tea ceremony as it is still performed today, was codified by Sen no Rikyu, a tea master who lived in the second half of the sixteenth century and who brought an almost liturgical ritualization to the ceremony.

Making food easier to digest

In prehistoric times, the essential mission of men and women was to survive; they were subject to the absolute necessity of finding enough food to expand their populations and to make a place for themselves in a hostile world. The diet of our earliest ancestors was largely plant-based. However, early vestiges attest that they frequently ate meat products that were high in protein, either from animals that had been hunted or from chance carrion. Fresh meat is hard to cut up and even harder to chew and digest. Fermentation, which tenderizes meat and makes it easier to chew, was probably one of the earliest techniques of food processing mastered by our Paleolithic ancestors. This method of pre-cooking transforms the nutritional properties of meat and makes its proteins easier for humans to assimilate. The word "ferment" comes from the Latin verb *fervere*, meaning "to boil," which illustrates how, in ancient times, this process was compared to a cooking method without fire.

Fermentation enables meat to be conserved for far longer than if it is merely cooked or eaten raw, particularly if it is finely sliced and sun-dried, a practice that began very early. In fact, traces of elephant quartering from as early as the Acheulean era, about 500,000 years ago, have been found in Spain.[19] What were hunters to do with the meat from such a huge beast? The solution to the question probably led to the first techniques of meat preservation that involved fermentation. Meat begins by fermenting when lactic acid helps the lactic flora naturally present on meat to grow. The meat is then dried in the sun and either ground to powder or smoked to ensure long conservation. All these techniques are still used to make jerky, the dried beef so popular in the US.
Preserving offal such as the stomach and intestines, which go off quickly, involves stuffing the intestines used as casing, then lactic fermentation, followed by drying.

Haggis is a dish that exemplifies this technique. The Scottish specialty is made of the sheep's stomach stuffed with lung, liver, and other mutton offal mixed with oatmeal and seasoning. This hunting dish, which used to be fermented, is a savory pudding (the word "pudding" comes to us from the Latin *botellus*, which means "small sausage" or "casing," as in the natural casing of a sausage) and is a legacy of a distant era. This is borne out in Book XVIII of the Odyssey, when Antinous mentions a similar dish:

Fermentation, which tenderizes meat and makes it easier to chew, was probably one of the earliest techniques of food processing mastered by our Paleolithic ancestors.

"Antinous, Eupeithes' son, proclaimed, 'Listen to what I have to say. There are goats' paunches filled with blood and fat, there by the fire ready for roasting, waiting for our dinner.'" [20]

Salt is known to have been used as early as Neolithic times. Salt makes curing possible, and curing is of course still practiced today to prepare ham, dried sausages, *pastirma* from Eastern Europe and the Levant, not to mention all sorts of other charcuterie widely found throughout the world. The concentration of salt prevents certain strains of bacteria from developing so that lactic acid bacteria can multiply. Lactic bacteria transform sugar (glucose) into lactic acid, thus acidifying the food and preventing dangerous bacteria from developing. Ham has been preserved using this method since antiquity. It is first salted and then dried until it has lost a good deal of its water. It is then matured in a cellar to encourage the lactic flora to develop. Dried sausages bear their recipe in their name: *salsus* is Latin for "salted." Dried sausage is the descendent of prehistoric stuffed stomach: casing stuffed with both fatty and lean meat that is chopped and brined; salt, sugar, and spices are added to encourage the development of the lactic bacteria and Micrococcaceae that allow fermentation to take place. This happens during the drying phase.

MULTIPLE FERMENTATIONS

Fermentation is a natural biochemical procedure enabling a raw foodstuff to be transformed by the enzymes produced by microorganisms. These microorganisms may be found in or on the food itself, as is the case with bacteria present in raw milk. They enable lactic fermentation to take place, transforming the milk into cheese. Most of the time, this process is usually anaerobic—it takes place in the absence of oxygen—and activates bacteria that produce the enzymes responsible for transforming organic compounds and fungi like mold as well as yeasts, which are unicellular fungi, such as the one that causes bread to rise as it produces carbonic gas.

There are several types of fermentation. Among the most widespread, let us mention:
• Alcoholic fermentation, which takes place naturally when fruit ripens too much, and which transforms the sugar into alcohol.
• Lactic fermentation, which transforms glucose into lactic acid when there is no air. This is the acid that comes into play to make yogurt, cheeses, and other fermented milk-derived products, as well as in charcuterie and fermented fish products like fish sauce. Lactic fermentation also takes place when vegetables are fermented. An example is sauerkraut, which is found throughout the Eurasian continent. There are other types of fermentation, such as acetic fermentation, which transforms alcohol into vinegar, and butyric fermentation, which produces the rancid taste of the tea with yak butter of which Tibetans are so fond.

Preserving and gathering: a constant problem

As fermentation techniques were mastered, it became possible to store larger amounts of food supplies. This in turned led to population growth among the first tribes. The process was also helped by the increasing sedenterization of tribes. Stocks of essential foods increased and so more people could be fed. This was a prelude to the establishment of the first villages.[21] The Neolithic revolution, which began in about 11,000 BCE in the Fertile Crescent in the Near East, was enabled by the social changes born of emerging sedentarization. Grain farming and cattle herding, together with the invention of pottery, combined with fermentation to increase supplies and to provide protection for the first village societies, which were somewhat fragile. We can therefore truly say that fermentation preceded and explains the Neolithic Revolution.[22] Grains were quickly transformed into flatbreads, then, with the help of leavening, into bread. Leavening is nothing more than a paste made of flour and water that has been left to ferment. A rich microcosm of lactic bacteria and yeasts develops in the paste, and this is how dough can be seeded and made to rise.

But the fermentation practiced in the Neolithic period was not only used for grains. Very early on, high-protein foods and those that spoil quickly, such as fish, were preserved using innovative fermentation techniques. Since salt was rare, costly, and less frequently used in the remote regions of Northern Europe such as Scandinavia, preserving fish posed a number of problems. These were resolved by experimenting with preparations that involved lower concentrations of salt. The techniques can be traced back to the eighth millennium BCE in southern Sweden[23] and are still used to today in dishes such as gravlax. The name of this fermented salmon means "buried salmon" (from *gräva*, "tomb"), an allusion to the fact that Scandinavian fishermen prepared their fish by salting it and placing it in large jars that were then buried in the sand. There, shielded from air, lactic fermentation took place. This allowed large catches that could not have been consumed or otherwise preserved to be kept for long periods. Another advantage was that the food was stored out of reach of predators. Carl von Linné, the famous Swedish naturalist, wrote in 1734 in his *A Tour in Lapland*, that in Dalarna "in spring, the people of Sarnâs salt the fish in its own blood and bury it."

Improvement

Fermentation not only preserves foods; another of its advantages is to transform naturally poisonous foods into edible foods. It is thus a precious process for survival in extreme conditions, when food resources are scarce and humans are reduced to consuming potentially dangerous foods. The Viking communities living in Iceland were able to survive in the dark of the boreal winter only by consuming highly toxic foodstuffs rendered harmless through fermentation. An example is *hákarl*, the fermented flesh of the Greenland shark. This shark lives at depths greater than 200 meters; its flesh is saturated with urea and trimethylamine N-oxide (TMAO), a powerful neurotoxin that protects it against the extreme water pressure of its habitat. When these sharks were beached on the Icelandic coasts, or when they were fished for the copious oil contained in their livers, it would have been a great loss, given the context of food scarcity, to let such an enormous amount of meat rot. To counter this toxicity, Icelandic people would first bury the flesh in the sand. By depriving it of air, they activated the reproduction of lactic bacteria as well as those of the Moraxella and Acinetobacter bacteria groups. The resulting fermentation gradually changed the urea and TMAO rate. Fermentation was followed by drying below wide awnings, with the Atlantic winds blowing over the flesh for nearly seventy days before the food became comestible. The end product, white flesh surrounded by a golden crust, was a food that the Icelanders considered as representing their longevity. *Hákarl* is still a symbol of Iceland and the determination of its people to survive in a hostile environment. Its strong smell of ammonia, a result of the transformation of urea by fermentation, and its taste, that some compare to the strongest Stilton or Roquefort cheeses, mask an otherwise inedible food that has been transformed into a healthy product.

Eating fermented foods thus provides nutrients during the winter season, when fresh produce cannot be harvested.

Health benefits

Consuming fermented foods is good for our health. And from Roman antiquity until Louis XIV's army, in France soldiers were fed on a daily grain ration known as *fromentée*,[24] a fermented, nourishing buckwheat porridge. The staple food of peasants was millet porridge, replaced in the seventeenth century by polenta, a porridge made of corn, the cereal that was brought back from the New World and known in southern Europe as "Spanish millet."[25]

Foods that have undergone lactic fermentation play an important role in the gut microbiome, essential for our health and immune system. An example is sauerkraut and other lacto-fermented vegetables which are found worldwide, such as Korean kimchi (which means "soaked vegetables"), comprising cabbage, radishes, and other vegetables that are fermented in large jars with chili peppers. The salt used to cover the vegetables inhibits pathogens and promotes the development of a rich microflora where the bacteria of lactic acid naturally present on vegetables predominate. Deprived of oxygen, the preparation acidifies, blocks the formation of pathogenic bacteria, and enables long preservation while keeping the nutritional properties of the food, its fibers, vitamins (particularly Vitamin C), calcium, iron, etc.

Eating fermented foods thus provides nutrients during the winter season, when fresh produce cannot be harvested. There are countless variations found worldwide, from the fermented vine leaves of the Balkans to the brined *malossol* and *kiszone* gherkins of the Slavic countries, from the achars of the Indian Ocean to the *tsukemono* of Japan.

The nutrients preserved by pickling can be used to treat and prevent certain diseases, most importantly scurvy, the dreaded curse of the sailors caused by a Vitamin C deficiency. During the early modern period, the diet of sailors on long voyages consisted mainly of ship's biscuit, or hardtack, and cured foods that contained very little ascorbic acid. After three months of sailing without fresh food, scurvy would wreak its harm on the men, often leading to death. In fact, scurvy was often the most important cause of death among European navies. In 1734, James Lind, a Scottish doctor, found that there was a correlation between a lack of fresh vegetables and the onset of scurvy.[26] It was believed at the time that acidity provided protection against the disease. But when James Cook learned that the Dutch, who travelled to the Dutch East Indies with sauerkraut on board, were less affected by the disease, he decided to do the same for his three voyages. By including sauerkraut and grogs containing lemon juice in the ship's diet, and including daily exercise in the routine, Cook succeeded in keeping his men from the cursed disease, which often killed over half of the crews.[27]

A striking example illustrates the influence of fermentation on our health: the lactose tolerance found among certain human populations.

A striking example illustrates the influence of fermentation on our health: the lactose tolerance found among certain human populations. Today, only part of the world's population can assimilate milk, thanks to lactase, an enzyme in the small intestine that breaks down lactose into glucose and galactose. The enzyme is found in all humans at birth, but its efficacy diminishes after the infant is weaned, making assimilation of milk difficult for the peoples whose lactase does not last into adult age, as was the case for prehistoric populations. Traces of the domestication of cattle and the use of dairy products have been found as far back as 10,500 BCE.[28] These dairy products, like yoghurts and cheeses, were products of milk fermentation, which uses lactic bacteria to transform lactose into lactic acid, making these foods perfectly edible even by adults with very little active lactase. The earliest traces of the consumption of fermented milk in the form of cheese date back to the sixth millennium BCE in Poland and Croatia,[29] but the first truly sizeable cheese-making operations appeared in the Sumerian Near East. Cheeses made in Europe require less salt because of the cooler climate. This means less acidity, which in turn encourages

the development of bacteria and molds responsible for a wide variety of tastes and textures. Back in 65 CE, Columella, a Roman farmer and writer, wrote on the subject in his treatise *De re rustica* (On Agriculture). While the English word "cheese" comes from the Latin *caseus*, as does the Spanish *queso*, the French word "fromage," has a different root: it comes from the Low Latin *formaticus*, which refers to the molded shape of the wide variety of cheeses already familiar to the Romans.

A FERMENT OF CIVILIZATION

Common values and culture

As the process of fermentation has been embraced by almost every culture for millennia, it cannot be separated from civilization. The word "culture," used to designate a set of values and common spiritual, intellectual, and artistic references, comes from the Latin word *colere* (to tend or cultivate) and is thus imbued with farming references. This is no coincidence. Food, and first and foremost fermented food, transmits a culture from the earliest stages of life, even before language is learned. It is no exaggeration, therefore, to consider fermented food to be the cultural foundation of a civilization as it enables a people to adapt to their natural environment and thus survive in extreme conditions.

The tragic history of the Vikings of Greenland is a telling example. Around 980 CE, the Vikings arrived in south-east Greenland from Iceland to take advantage of the favorable conditions resulting from the Medieval Warm Period. They enlarged villages and even built their own cathedral in their main settlement, Gardar, which was a bishop's seat until 1400. They subsisted by hunting local species such as the walrus, whose valuable tusks were exported to Norway, but primarily by raising cows, sheep, and goats imported from Scandinavia. The livestock were used more for their milk than for their meat. The milk was transformed into cheese, butter, and skyr, made by heating milk in a vat to activate fermentation. It was then strained to achieve the consistency of a thick yogurt, but one that kept very well at ambient temperature.[30] These fermented foods were consumed during the long, arduous Arctic winter and the animals, the most precious possessions of these inhabitants of Greenland, were the focus of all their care and attention. The Vikings reproduced the way of life they had led in Scandinavia, producing their own fermented foods in an environment that was far more hostile than the one they had left. When, early in the fourteenth century, the Little Ice Age followed the Medieval Warm Period, basic conditions became far harsher and new inhabitants, the proto-Inuit, who had been living in Canada until then, appeared when they had to leave the High Arctic because of the worsening cold. Their lifestyle was far more suited to low temperatures than that of the Vikings. They could move about easily and hunted ringed seal and whales; most importantly, they fermented their kill to make provisions for winter, which gave them a decided advantage over the Vikings, who depended almost entirely on their cattle for survival. All the Inuit needed to do to condemn the Vikings to starvation was to burn their barns in winter. These factors are the likely explanation of the disappearance of Viking settlements in Greenland in the fifteenth century. Those fierce, proud conquerors who nothing and no one could withstand were eventually overcome by a food crisis caused by transposing their Scandinavian mode of life too directly to an environment that was not suitable for it.[31]

Food, and first and foremost fermented food, transmits a culture from the earliest stages of life, even before language is learned.

The preparation and consumption of the essential foodstuff that is the basis of the diet of a civilization strengthens the bonds that unite local communities. This is the case of Korean kimchi, which is made of cabbage and other lacto-fermented vegetables and stored in large jars. In late fall, villagers would get together to prepare the winter kimchi without which they could not survive the cold season. The ritualized event became a festive occasion of great cultural importance, meaning that kimchi constituted an indispensable tie within the Korean civilization.[32] The same type of social phenomena is found in Europe, such as grape harvesting and wine-making in wine-producing regions.

ATTRACTION AND REPULSION

As we have seen, each civilization bases its food culture on one or several fermented foodstuffs that are integral to their lives. Therein lies the origin of a liking or distaste for a category of foodstuffs or dishes. Fermented soy sauce, rice wine, and *doubanjiang*, a spicy paste of fermented soybeans, explain the specific taste of Chinese cuisine. These ingredients are indispensable to Chinese people living in the diaspora, but anyone for whom they are not a cultural and dietary staple will be uninterested in them. French people, who have grown up with raw milk cheeses, full of texture and aromas, that fill supermarket refrigerators and grocery stores, sorely miss them if they emigrate. But to Asians and Americans, their smell and taste may be unbearable and they might well crack jokes about them. Claude Lévi-Strauss recounts that in 1944 when the Americans landed in Normandy, the GIs mistook the cellars where Camembert cheeses were ripened for premises where corpses were rotting after massacres had been perpetrated there. They burned dairies because they thought they reeked of dead bodies. For him, this was a clear distinction between the French and the allies: for the French, cheeses are alive. They do not decompose; they breathe.[33]

A famous Chinese specialty is *pidan*, century eggs, also known as hundred- and thousand-year eggs. Asian gourmets rave about them while tourists reel in horror. These fermented duck eggs are stored in ashes or coated in rice bran for about a month to activate the transformation of the yolk, which turns green and gains a stronger taste, while the white takes on a gelatinous consistency and turns amber. Another specialty for adventurous gourmets is *surströmming*, the fermented herring so emblematic of Sweden. It is made of small herrings caught in

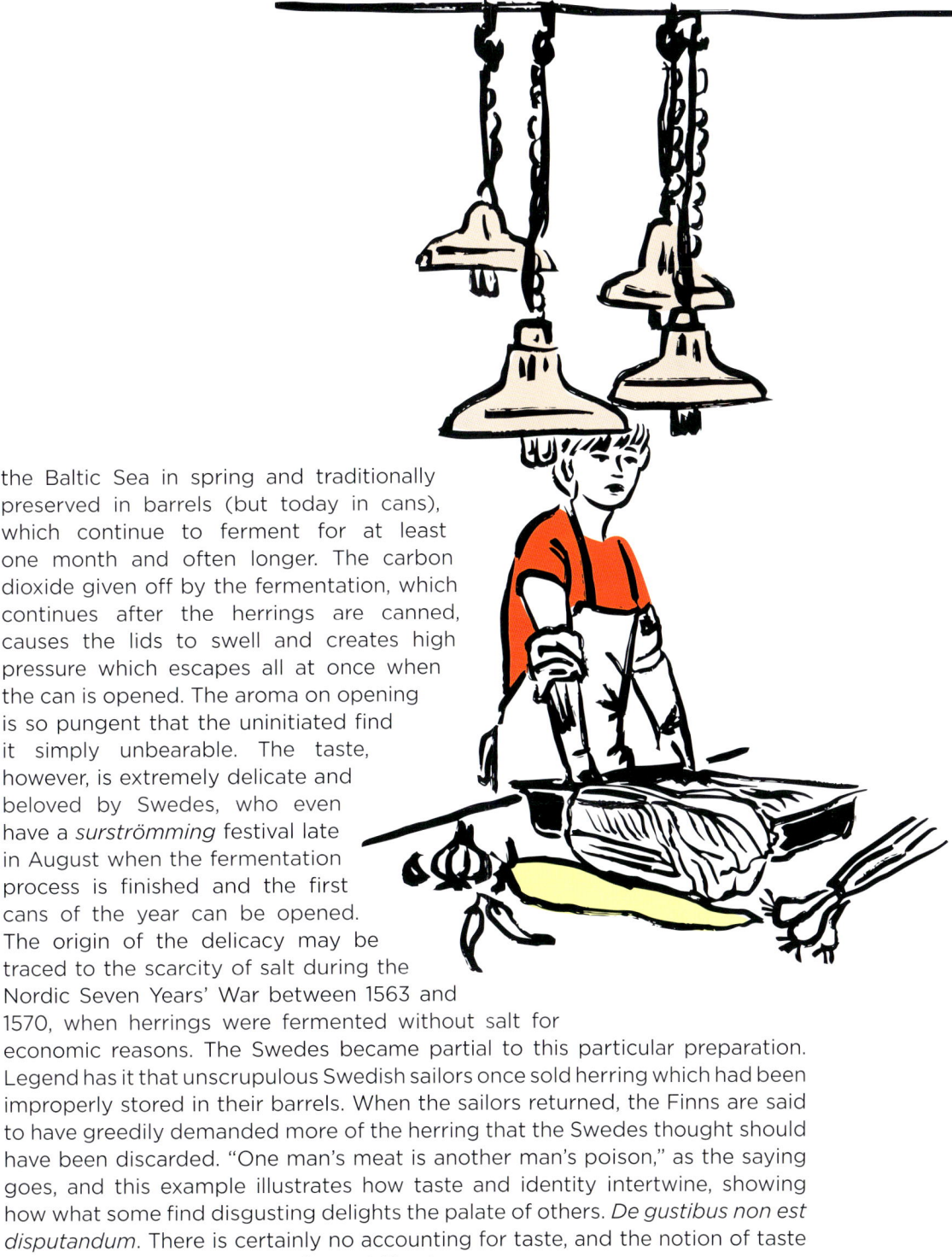

the Baltic Sea in spring and traditionally preserved in barrels (but today in cans), which continue to ferment for at least one month and often longer. The carbon dioxide given off by the fermentation, which continues after the herrings are canned, causes the lids to swell and creates high pressure which escapes all at once when the can is opened. The aroma on opening is so pungent that the uninitiated find it simply unbearable. The taste, however, is extremely delicate and beloved by Swedes, who even have a *surströmming* festival late in August when the fermentation process is finished and the first cans of the year can be opened. The origin of the delicacy may be traced to the scarcity of salt during the Nordic Seven Years' War between 1563 and 1570, when herrings were fermented without salt for economic reasons. The Swedes became partial to this particular preparation. Legend has it that unscrupulous Swedish sailors once sold herring which had been improperly stored in their barrels. When the sailors returned, the Finns are said to have greedily demanded more of the herring that the Swedes thought should have been discarded. "One man's meat is another man's poison," as the saying goes, and this example illustrates how taste and identity intertwine, showing how what some find disgusting delights the palate of others. *De gustibus non est disputandum*. There is certainly no accounting for taste, and the notion of taste takes us back to the origins of our civilizations.

The Mediterranean triad, or the seeds of a civilization

Taste is one of the solid foundations of civilizations, most likely because it results from the eating habits inherent to the dominant cultures of a human group. The Mediterranean triad—the cultivation of wheat, grapes, and olives—gave rise to the food triptych of bread-wine-oil on which the Greco-Roman food civilization was built and from which European food habits have largely stemmed.

This triad, which includes two fermented foodstuffs, was the symbolic basis of the Greco-Roman diet. For them, bread, wine, and oil were above all the markers of civilization, enabling a distinction to be made between the civilized and the uncivilized. For the Greeks, anyone who did not speak Greek was a barbarian; for them, the language of such people was an incomprehensible babble of sounds like "bar bar," giving rise to the name of *barbaros*, meaning "babbler." It is worth noting that bara means "bread" in Breton. The word is linked to the French word *baragouin*, which first appeared late in the Middle Ages and which was updated and became popular after the Franco-Prussian War of 1870–71, when there was a great mixing of the peoples of the various regions of France. Breton soldiers passing through would ask for *bara* (bread) and *gwin* (wine). This amusing coincidence underlines just how integral these two fermented foodstuffs were to the Latin civilization and its descendants. The Roman Empire moved the cursor of civilization from language to food. The many peoples who made up the Empire did not share the same language and the governing powers recognized two official languages, Latin in the west and Greek in the east. So, it was the consumption of the ancient triad of bread, wine, and oil that characterized the civilized person in Roman culture. Justin, a third-century Roman historian, maintained that one could become civilized by adopting this triad. Under the influence of the Phocaeans, "the barbarian ways [of the Gauls] being laid aside and also softened; … they learned to prune the vine and to plant the olive."[34] And in fact, Romanized Gauls bred the grape varieties that were most resistant to the cold, which meant that vines could be grown widely in Europe.

In Ancient Greece, most notably in Homer's *Odyssey*, anyone who is an eater of bread is a mortal. But for bread to rise, spontaneous fermentation of the dough is not enough. It must be mixed with starter to make delicious, light loaves. In Douanne, Switzerland, a perfectly preserved risen bread dating back to between 3560 to 3530 BCE was found. Although mainly starter was used to leaven dough, it appears that the Egyptians were the first to use yeast from beer produced in the same workshops as bread, around 1500 BCE.[35] For both symbolic and dietary reasons, the ancient Mediterranean diet gave bread pride of place. The diet of the Roman soldier is evidence of this reality: consuming between 1¾ and 2¼ lb. (0.8–1 kg) of wheat daily,[36] he was first and foremost an eater of bread. Because bread is compact, it is easy to transport, keeps without rotting, and is high in nutritional value. It is also considered to be the most nutritious food. It was the universal foodstuff of ancient Rome and had an important social aspect—it was found in all classes of Roman society. Bakeries were numerous (in Pompei, where the population was between twelve and fifteen thousand, thirty-three bakeries were found) and produced a profusion of risen breads of very different shapes and tastes. There were loaves stamped with the baker's name, brioche-type milk breads, and breads flavored with cumin, mushrooms, sage, cheese, and more.[37] A noteworthy custom is that of euergetism, a practice of public generosity that played a significant role in society. The best-known example is *panem et circenses* (bread and circuses), which symbolizes the central place bread held in the Roman social system.

For both symbolic and dietary reasons, the ancient Mediterranean diet gave bread pride of place.

Bread was pivotal in the Middle Ages, sacralized by the Christian religion, and the staple foodstuff of all social classes. In France, under Louis XIV, the poorer people of Paris ate around 3 lb. (1.5 kg) of bread per person on a daily basis.[38] King Louis XVI was nicknamed the "Baker King," and the figure of the monarch as provider of bread became the symbol of a social contract between the king and the towns. The taste of bread changed and increasingly became an important social marker. In the seventeenth century, and even more so in the eighteenth, whiter, lighter bread was increasingly sought after; it became accordingly more costly. The coveted fluffy, light white bread known as *pain mollet* (softish bread) and *pain à la reine* (queen's bread, so named when Marie de' Medici became fond of it) was made not with starter but with yeast.[39]

The color and texture of bread are not only defining elements, but also a distinctive sign of civilization, as Goethe mentions when he recounts a memorable event he experienced in 1792 in his *Campaign in France in the Year 1792*. He felt pity for two ravenous young French peasants and offered to share with them the *pain de munition* (soldier's bread ration) that he had bought from hussars. To his surprise, the two Frenchmen refused to touch it, claiming that all they ate was, "*De bon pain, de bonne soupe, de bonne viande, de bonne bière*" (good bread, good soup, good meat, good beer). Goethe drew his conclusion about this marker of civilization, "White and black bread is properly ... the battle cry, between Germans and French."[40] As the chef Paul Bocuse expressed it, "cuisine can . . . sometimes be used as propaganda. . . . Some countries even use it as a means of gaining recognition."[41]

How ferment migrates and travels

A fermented foodstuff is a symbol of a community and as such may represent, for travelers, their culture of origin that they transpose into the new territories where they settle. For example, in the eighteenth century, Californian vineyards were planted by Spanish missionaries, who needed wine for their liturgical ceremonies. The same is true of Argentina and Chile. Bread has a more complex history. Bread developed in various forms on just about every continent—the Chinese *mantou*, a crustless steamed white bun, and Turkish pita are two examples of this. But the omnipresence of Western-style leavened bread, which from the early seventeenth century onward comprised up to 90 percent of the food consumed by Europeans, as well as its symbolically charged value, meant that European bread has spread worldwide. American trappers travelled with their own leavening that had often originated in Europe and created European-style bread adapted to the climate and environment of their new homeland. Similarly, Vietnamese *bánh mì*, which literally means "buckwheat bread" is French baguette that the nineteenth-century colonizers took to Indochina. In an adaptation to the local climate, the bread is not crusty but has retained the shape of the French specialty. The name *bánh mì* refers to both the baguette and the sandwich made from it. It was originally a simple copy of the typically French butter-and-ham sandwich (*jambon-beurre*), but was adapted to Vietnamese cuisine and condiments and has become a specialty in its own right, a symbol of the country.

A fermented foodstuff is a symbol of a community and as such may represent, for travelers, their culture of origin.

Other migrations remain more mysterious. This is the case of Roman *garum* and South East Asian *nuoc mam*. Which one influenced the other? Was there any influence at all? Could they merely have been developed at the same time, using the same product and practically the same recipe? Both are fermented sauces made through autolysis, "the auto-digestion of the fish by the enzymes in its own digestive tract"[42] to which a lactic ferment is added. *Garum* was a central element of Roman cooking, used as a condiment for all their dishes; *allec*, the fish paste from which *garum* was made, was widely consumed by laborers and peasants with their bread. The Romans imported it into all the countries of their Empire and, like wine, it was to be found on every dining table. There were certainly low-priced common grades of *garum*, but the *garum* of blood, made with the gills and viscera of red tuna or mackerel, and especially the *garum sociorum* (garum of the allies) produced in Baetica, southern Spain, fetched high prices.[43] *Garum and allec* continued to be produced in southern Europe throughout the Middle Ages and then in the Byzantine Empire. The Turkish *rajihe* and *pissalat* from the city of Nice—derived, quite simply, from *peis salat* (salted fish)—are condiments that have come down to us from this era.[44] *Pissalat* is the name of a fermented paste of anchovies and sardines. The famous *pissaladière*, an anchovy tart which is a specialty of Nice and Liguria, is very similar to the bread spread with *allec* that Roman laborers liked so much. Provencal *anchoïade* and *colatura di alici* from Amalfi are close relatives.

Sadly, it is impossible to say if *garum* and *nuoc mam* have a common ancestor, or if one or the other traveled along the ancient Silk Road. But what is certain is that Worcestershire sauce, fermented for eighteen months before it is used as a seasoning for steaks and Bloody Mary cocktails, originated with a Bengali fish sauce brought back from British India and then produced in Worcester, England. Similarly, ketchup, according to Andrew F. Smith, from the name *ke-tsiap*, a word from a southern Chinese dialect, referred to a sauce that was identical to *nuoc mam*. It was eaten in Indonesia and became immensely popular in eighteenth-century England, where, around 1800, it was modified with the addition of tomatoes. After the anchovies were removed, it became the ketchup we know today that is used to dip French fries in the world over.[45]

WHEN YEAST EXTRACT PROVIDED A SUBSTITUTE FOR MEAT

In 1892 the first stock cube made with meat extract was launched. And very soon the producers hit on an idea: they could transform yeasts into a food that resembled meat in both taste and appearance. Many competitors entered the market in a race to make it. In 1902, Marmite was born. The savory spread is made from yeast used to ferment beer and is an excellent source of proteins and vitamins. It tastes like meat but contains none. The economical creation soon won the hearts of the British, and during World War II, tons of Marmite were sent to the soldiers at the front to help them overcome the lack of meat.

PASTEURIZATION, DECLINE, AND A NEW BEGINNING

The decline

With the nineteenth century and its enthusiasm for technical progress and avid hunger for science, the attitude to food preservation techniques dating back thousands of years changed. Such preparations were the result of the experiments, experience, and practice of countless generations.

The method of canning invented in 1795 by Nicolas Appert, a candy maker turned wholesaler from Paris, sterilizes food to destroy not only disease-causing bacteria but also those responsible for fermentation. The procedure he used was called *appertisation* in French to honor the inventor of the canning procedure. Appert's discovery owed everything to empiricism. The process of pasteurization, on the other hand, owed nothing to chance. While working in the city of Lille in northern France, Louis Pasteur developed the theory of the role of living microorganisms in fermentation. Around 1860, he also proved that microorganisms appear and grow not by spontaneous generation but through the spores present both on food and in the air. This validated the theory that certain microbes are responsible for contagious diseases. Pasteurization, which involves heating a food to between 144 and 190°F (62 and 88°C) for a given time, destroys the bacteria without altering its organoleptic qualities and thus extends its shelf life. Thanks to pasteurization, fresh milk, which only keeps for a few hours when it has been milked, can be stored for one to two weeks after undergoing the process. The technique is helped by refrigeration and freezing, which also extend the shelf life of fresh produce.

Although the hygienist movement in the West over the nineteenth and twentieth centuries tended to mean that fermented foods were relegated to traditional societies, science and fermentation are by no means diametrically opposed. On the contrary, it is thanks to studying fermentation that physics, chemistry, and medicine progressed in leaps and bounds. In the late eighteenth century, Antoine Lavoisier, a French nobleman and chemist, discovered that when sugar undergoes alcoholic fermentation, it decomposes into alcohol and CO_2.[46]

Lavoisier's research presages that of Charles Cagniard de Latour, who in 1838 described yeast as being living matter, as well as that of Pasteur, who in 1857 showed that yeast functions like a living organism. In 1854, Pasteur was appointed dean of the University of Lille. There he studied subjects that were of interest to the chemical industry. An example was his study of the alcoholic fermentation of beet sugar, undertaken through the father of one of his students, Monsieur Bigo, who had a distillery that was located in the Wazemmes neighborhood of Lille.[47]

While working in the city of Lille in northern France, Louis Pasteur developed the theory of the role of living microorganisms in fermentation.

It is clear that studying fermentation led to decisive scientific progress, but science itself also sought to improve or at least to optimize the fermentation process. Again, it was Pasteur who, affected by France's 1870 defeat in the Franco-Prussian War and the fall of his protector, Napoleon III, decided to ensure that French beer became a true competitor of the German beer that was enjoying such a boom. His research demonstrated that with top fermentation (the process of fermenting ales and certain other alcoholic beverages from the top of the fermenting liquid), the yeast was contaminated by the environment in the brewery. Beers quickly turn sour and are hard to store for long periods. Pasteur suggested producing beer in a controlled environment with the least possible contact with air during fermentation and pasteurization (heating to 150°F [65°C] for 20 minutes) in the bottle to stabilize the drink and prevent fermentation from continuing. *The bière de la revanche*[48] (beer of revenge) that he created could be shipped, stored, and produced in large quantities, transforming French beer-brewing into a powerful industry.

During the nineteenth century, the understanding of the phenomenon of fermentation meant that the most suitable ferments could be cultivated and selected to seed fermented products. Beer yeast, *Saccharomyces cerevisiae* (literally, the fungus of barley beer) was identified and cultivation of the pure strains began in dedicated vats. Before this discovery, bakers got their yeast from beer brewers. Yeast became a product in its own right, one that was industrially produced to supply bakers and pastry chefs, and when the Lesaffre group invented instant dry yeast in 1973, it was also available for home use. The same strain is used for wine-making. *Saccharomyces cerevisiae* is the most widely found yeast in wine-making: the addition of a selected yeast not only makes for faster, more stable, and more predictable fermentation, it also enables sheer tasting pleasure. Likewise, the improved knowledge and control of microorganisms gives Camembert cheese the appearance we know today. Before the twentieth century, both Camembert and Brie cheese had a greenish rind covered with red spots, due to the combined action of various microorganisms: *Penicillium camemberti*, which makes the rind white and downy, was often overpowered by a veritable army of molds whose spores lived in the cheese ripening cellars. In the late nineteenth century, biochemist Georges Roger, working for the makers of Brie de Meaux, isolated the strain responsible for the white color. Thanks to one of his former colleagues, this strain of white Penicillium was taken to Normandy, where it was used by Camembert makers to seed their cheeses, ensuring the finished product was immaculate.[49]

Fermentation makes its comeback

In the twenty-first century, society has somewhat tempered the excessive belief in scientific techniques of the two previous centuries. There is a marked trend toward rediscovering or reacquiring traditional food-making techniques, including the ancestral technique of fermentation. The development of organic farming, permaculture, and the enthusiasm for shortening supply chains all contribute to a general aspiration for better eating. The importance of the gut microbiome as well as the bacteria present in our bodies and our environment has been rediscovered and Western medicine has a new perspective on the benefits of certain microorganisms. Society has realized how importance diet is to health, to our very beings. "We are what we eat," as primatologist and anthropologist Jane Goodall says. And so, a return to natural, traditional ways has helped us rediscover fermentation, some of whose age-old techniques were on the verge of disappearing. Once again, the benefits of lacto-fermentation for digestion are appreciated, and jars of home-made fermented vegetables crowd the shelves of all those who are increasingly concerned about their health. Traditional foods have become nutraceuticals. Tastes are changing and the prophetically nostalgic phrase of philosopher Guy Debord for traditional foods that have been replaced by banal "hunger abators" (the antiquated French term is *abat-faim*), "There was taste, but not any more,"[50] resounds ever louder as we advance in the twenty-first century.

But now we want to eat the bread our forefathers ate—witness the popularity of sourdough bread. Unpasteurized beers are also growing in popularity, with hundreds of micro-breweries opening every year to offer us an ever-widening range of brews with increasingly sophisticated fermentations. So much so that the triumph of craft beers has led to real shortages of hops. We now let living matter take action: we eagerly quaff natural wines whose bottles sometimes don't require opening as the corks pop up on their own. DIY kits for beer and cheese are trendy in cities, where it is hardest to maintain a direct connection with nature.

The importance of the gut microbiome as well as the bacteria present in our bodies and our environment has been rediscovered.

Food localism, however, highlights a problem revealed by fermentation: you can't make Roquefort cheese in Japan, nor genuine sake in Zimbabwe. The environment simply doesn't permit it; the bacterial microclimate that enables these unique foods to be made cannot be reproduced. That is why the international homogenization of taste becomes wearying. We don't want to eat the same food from Paris to Tokyo. Bread must have a different taste in Bordeaux than in Shanghai.

Fermentation is humanity's oldest companion; it has acquired a new lease on life and thanks to its vitality, promises to enhance our meals for centuries to come.

THE MANY VARIETIES OF FERMENTED FOODS

Since the dawn of time, humans have unwittingly made use of fermentation. Today, we have adopted these fermentation techniques, applying them to all the great food groups: bread, drinks, fruit and vegetables, meat, and fish.

In this second part, we are going to look at the practical aspects of fermentation: how to make pickles, prepared with fresh vegetables; ginger beer, using fresh ginger; and simple buckwheat pancakes, made from just flour and water. But we are also going to provide the tools to understand more complicated processes that involve more advanced techniques, knowledge, or equipment, such as making bread, wine, and beer.

From this world of fermented foods, we have chosen the most iconic. In learning these basic techniques and gaining an understanding of the principles of fermentation, you will be opening a window onto a little-known aspect of gastronomy.

THE ICONIC PRODUCTS

Imagine a festive buffet table: for appetizers, slices of gravlax sit alongside slices of dried duck breast, while radish and carrot pickles are accompanied by a tangy yogurt sauce. A sauerkraut takes center stage, surrounded by different types of sausage, ready to be served with a spicy sauce. In the kitchen, pancake batter is waiting to be turned into dessert when the time comes. Everything here is fermented: vegetables, meat and fish, dairy, cereals, and sauces. A wealth of possibilities to discover.

FERMENTED VEGETABLES: PLENTY OF SCOPE FOR THE IMAGINATION

Fermenting vegetables is no recent fad. Indeed, before the advent of the refrigerator and sterilization, this was the only way to conserve them. Today, fermented vegetables are making a comeback, mainly due to the distinctive flavor they develop and the infinite range of possibilities they offer. In fact, any vegetables that can be eaten raw can be fermented, combined with herbs or spices, and enjoyed. The only limit is your imagination! What is more, fermented vegetables are very healthy.

Lactic fermentation

When vegetables are fermented, they acidify. Good bacteria, aided by salt and the absence of air, convert the sugar that is naturally present in the vegetables into lactic acid. These good bacteria cancel out the bad bacteria and begin to break down the fibers in fruits and vegetables. The result: crunchy, tangy, fresh vegetables that are very good for the health.

How to encourage vegetable fermentation
Fermentation in brine (salt diluted in water) is most suitable for vegetables that do not contain much water, such as olives, carrots, and pickles. By contrast, salt without water enables you to ferment vegetables with a high water content, such as cabbage and fennel.

Preparing your own fermented vegetables

Ingredients

Vegetables
Always choose organic vegetables, because the idea is to activate the bacteria already present on the vegetables and so you don't want to wash them too much.

Salt
Choose unrefined salt—such as gray coarse salt or Himalayan pink salt—because it is rich in mineral salts and trace elements, some of which encourage the growth of good bacteria. In general, when fermenting vegetables using only salt, you should use 1 percent salt, or 1 scant teaspoon of salt per pound of vegetables (10 g per 1 kg). When fermenting in brine, you will need 3 percent salt, or 1 tablespoon salt per 2 cups of water (30 g per liter).

Water (for the brine)
You can use any sort of water, provided it is not overly chlorinated. If your water is quite chlorinated, let it rest for an hour before beginning the fermentation.

What you need to know to ensure successful fermentation

• The vegetables need to be completely covered with the brine. If they float to the surface, place a weight on top, for example a squeezed lemon or a cabbage stalk that is too hard to use. You could also keep them submerged using two crossed toothpicks (cocktail sticks) or a plastic bag filled with brine. Be careful not to fill the jar to the brim, or the carbon dioxide released by the vegetables may cause the liquid to overflow.
• The jar needs to be well sealed; if it isn't, bad bacteria can create mold.
• During the first week, keep the vegetables at room temperature, between 59 and 77°F (15 to 25°C). Bacteria, like yeast, love temperate environments. Then, move them to the fridge to slow down the fermentation process.

Preserving fermented vegetables

If they are kept in the fridge, and the jar is unopened, the vegetables will keep for 5 to 18 months. Cabbage, carrots, and beet, for example, will stay firm and keep a long time, whereas radishes and cucumber tend to go soft quicker. Either way, the vegetables won't become toxic, they'll just lose some of their consistency and flavor.

FERMENTING FOOD WITH SALT

SAUERKRAUT

With its tangy taste and distinctive flavor, sauerkraut is one of the top national dishes in Germany, where people gather to eat it and enjoy a good meal and lively conversation. Making your own sauerkraut could be a great way to have an enjoyable evening with friends or family, so why not give it a try?

Equipment
- A jar for the cabbage
- Gloves, if you wish, because the salt can hurt your fingers

Ingredients
- A cabbage, preferably organic; white is most common, but it will taste just as good with red (allow 9 oz./250 g of sauerkraut per person)
- Unrefined salt; the quantity will depend on the weight of your cabbage
- Juniper berries

SAUERKRAUT IS CHINESE

In the third century BCE, laborers were busy on the ramparts of the Great Wall of China. It was cold and they were a long way from home. They had brought cabbage with them, but forgotten about, it began to ferment. Fortunately, they realized that this fermented cabbage was actually very good: sauerkraut was born, and it fed them over many long months. However, it was not until much later, in the sixteenth century, that the Germans mastered fermentation using salt and prepared sauerkraut as we know it today.

1. Rinse the cabbage very briefly under the tap. The more you wash it, the more of the bacteria on the cabbage you will remove. Remove the two outermost leaves; they will serve as a wedge to keep the cabbage submerged in the liquid.

2. Cut the cabbage into quarters, discarding the stalk, then weigh it. Cut it into thin slices. Add 1 scant teaspoon of salt per pound of cabbage (2 teaspoons per kilo) and leave to draw for about an hour to facilitate the next step.

3. Put on your gloves, if using. Mix the cabbage and salt. Massage firmly to break down the fibers so that they release as much water as possible. When you have finished, the cabbage should be bathing in liquid. Tip in the juniper berries and mix again.

4. Transfer the cabbage to a glass jar, pushing it down with your fist to remove as much air as possible.

5. When the cabbage is well compacted, wedge it in place with the two reserved outer leaves and use a weight to keep it submerged in the liquid. This could be a glass weight, a piece of cabbage stalk, or a plastic bag filled with brine. Make sure, too, that you leave a space between the cabbage and the lid so that the juice doesn't overflow. Seal tightly.

6. Let ferment for 1 week at room temperature, then 2 weeks in the fridge. Once opened, the sauerkraut should be consumed within 3 to 4 weeks. Left unopened, the jar can be kept a year in a cool place or in the fridge.

The tangy taste of sauerkraut makes it a good match for the sausages and charcuterie that traditionally accompany it. The freshness of the lactic acid cuts through the fat of the meat and aids digestion.

FERMENTING FOOD WITH SALT

KIMCHI
THE ALTERNATIVE TO SAUERKRAUT

In Korea, kimchi is more than a national dish, it's a way of life. Kimchi is everywhere: as a side, in stews, and in fried rice. There are hundreds of recipes for kimchi, which you can reinterpret as you wish (for example, by serving it with Korean noodles, as shown opposite).

Equipment
- A jar for the cabbage
- Gloves, if you wish, because the salt can hurt your fingers

Ingredients
- 1 napa cabbage
- Unrefined salt; the quantity will depend on the weight of your cabbage; allow 1.5 percent salt, or ½ tablespoon of salt per pound of cabbage (15 g per kilo). You can use more (but not more than ¾ tbsp) if you want to ferment the cabbage longer
- ½ daikon
- 3 carrots
- 4 green onions
- A few garlic chives
- 1 cup (½ pint/250 ml) water
- 1 tbsp potato or tapioca starch
- 1 tbsp brown sugar
- 10 garlic cloves
- 1 tbsp chopped fresh ginger
- ½ onion
- 4 tbsp (2 fl oz./60 ml) *nuoc mam* (fish sauce)
- 1 cup (3 ½ oz./100 g) *gochugaru* (Korean chili powder); you can use up to 2 cups (7 oz./200 g) for very hot cabbage or even 2 ½ cups (9 oz./250 g), if you're very brave!

1. As for sauerkraut, rinse the cabbage only briefly. Set aside the two outer leaves, then cut the cabbage into quarters. Combine it with the salt and let draw for 2 hours.

2. Cut the cabbage into fairly thick (about 4 in./10 cm) slices and place in a large mixing bowl. Wearing gloves, massage the cabbage slices well to soften them. The bottom of the bowl should be full of juice.

3. Finely chop the daikon, carrots, green onions, and garlic chives.

4. In a saucepan, heat the water, potato starch, and brown sugar until thick and gelatinous. Let cool.

5. Blend the garlic, ginger, onion, *nuoc mam*, and *gochugaru* and mix into the cooled potato starch mixture.

6. Add this chili paste to the cabbage and mix together well.

7. Using your hands, place the kimchi into the jar, pressing down well using your fist with each handful added. The idea is to remove the air and to pack the ingredients in as tightly as possible. As for sauerkraut, wedge the kimchi in place by covering it with the reserved cabbage leaves. You can also place a weight on top of the cabbage to ensure it stays immersed in the liquid.

8. Let ferment at room temperature for 1 week. You can then eat it immediately or place it in the fridge to slow down its fermentation. Kept closed, the jar will keep for 6 months; once opened, consume within a few weeks.

FERMENTING FOOD IN BRINE

PICKLES

Olives, cauliflower, carrot, all kinds of radish, broccoli, turnip, fennel, cucumber, garlic—the possibilities are endless. And you can flavor them as you wish with peppercorns, bay leaves, and all sorts of spices.

Equipment
- A jar

Ingredients
- Carrot, cauliflower, radish, etc.
- 4 ¼ cups (2 pints/1 liter) water
- 2 tbsp gray sea salt
- Herbs: thyme, laurel
- Freshly ground black pepper
- Spices

PICKLES AND CLEOPATRA

Cleopatra's secret to looking so young and beautiful: pickles! And Julius Caesar gave pickles to his soldiers to make them even stronger.

1. Briefly rinse the vegetables, then peel them and chop them into fairly large pieces.

2. Prepare the brine.

3. Place the vegetables in a jar, adding herbs and spices between each layer of vegetables. Press down firmly using your first to eliminate as much air as possible between each layer.

4. Pour the brine over the vegetables to cover them. If they float to the surface, try to keep them submerged in the brine using a weight, two crossed toothpicks (cocktail sticks) or a piece of vegetable.

5. Let ferment at room temperature for 1 week. You can then eat the pickles, but they will be even better after 2 weeks in the fridge.

As an appetizer, as a side to accompany a fairly substantial dish, in a salad, or in a sandwich: pickles add pep to the simplest of dishes.

FERMENTING FOOD IN BRINE

OLIVES

Unless you happen to live in an olive grove, the most difficult thing about preparing your own olives is getting hold of them. Though if you live in California or one of the southern states, or in Southern Europe, you may be able to find them in markets in season.

Equipment
- A 1-quart jar

Ingredients
- 2 lb. (900 g) fresh green or black olives
- 4 ¼ cups (2 pints/1 liter) water
- 2 tbsp gray sea salt
- Herbs: bay leaf, sprigs of fennel, thyme, rosemary, etc.

1. The first step is to make the olives less bitter. To do this, you need to soak them in a container of cold water for 8 to 15 days. Change the water daily and taste the olives regularly. When they are to your taste, place them in the jar.

2. In a saucepan, boil 4 ¼ cups (2 pints/1 liter) of water. Remove from the heat and add the salt and your choice of herbs. Let cool.

3. Pour the brine and herbs over the olives. Seal the jar tightly and store at room temperature. You will need to wait 4 to 6 months before eating them, but you can enjoy them for years after that!

Good to know: olives tend to go brown, but this is normal. The jars you buy from shops often contain additives to preserve the olives' original color.

MEAT AND FISH

The techniques for making saucisson, cured meat, and dried fish developed from the practice of hanging meat used by our distant *Australopithecus* cousins some three million years ago. While they had no choice (they had to let the meat tenderize before they could eat it), we have continued the practice because it enhances the flavor and texture of both fish and meat. And once again, these fermented foods often take pride of place on festive tables.

Lactic fermentation

The process responsible for fermenting vegetables and yogurts is also used to "cook" meat and fish. In this case, lactic fermentation requires salt, which, in contact with the meat or fish, dries it out and gives it its distinctive flavor. The salt causes large amounts of lactic acid bacteria to develop, preventing other less favorable bacteria from doing so.

FERMENTING WITH SALT

DRIED DUCK BREAST

Sliced very thinly, this dried duck breast is perfect as an appetizer or in a salad.

Equipment
- A glass dish
- A clean kitchen towel

Ingredients
For a 1 lb. 5 oz. (600 g) duck breast, which will serve 6 people
- 4 ½ cups (2 ¼ lb./1 kg) coarse salt
- Some thyme
- Some lightly crushed black pepper

1. Pour the salt into a glass dish, add the duck breast, and cover it with the salt. Press down on the duck breast so that it is firmly embedded in the salt. Cover the dish with a clean kitchen towel, place it in the fridge, and let rest for 12 hours.

2. After 12 hours, lightly rinse the duck breast with water, then dry it using paper towel.

3. Massage the thyme and crushed pepper into the duck breast.

4. Wrap the duck breast in a clean kitchen towel and place it in the coldest part of your fridge.

5. Leave in the fridge for at least 3 weeks, turning it over occasionally. The longer you leave it, the firmer and more flavorsome it will be.

SALMON GRAVLAX WITH DILL

Once you've tried this recipe, you'll never want to go back to ordinary smoked salmon. Packed in salt, the salmon slowly ferments. And you're in control of all the ingredients. With no additives and no preservatives, gravlax is all good!

Equipment
- Tweezers
- A large dish
- A weight or 1-quart (1-liter) bottle of milk

Ingredients
For 2 ¼ lb. (1 kg) salmon, which will serve 10 people
- ½ cup (3 ½ oz./100 g) coarse salt
- ½ cup (3 ½ oz./100 g) superfine sugar
- 1 tsp crushed white pepper
- 1 bunch dill
- 1 lime
- 3 tbsp (1 oz./30 g) pink peppercorns
- Olive oil

1. Ask your fishmonger to cut you two salmon fillets, each weighing 1 lb. 2 oz. (500 g), that you can lay on top of each other.

2. Three days before you want to eat the gravlax, remove the bones from the fillets using tweezers, then sprinkle the fish with the salt, sugar, and pepper. Cover the surface of one of the fillets with dill sprigs (leaving some for serving). Place the other fillet on top and wrap everything in plastic wrap.

3. Let macerate in the fridge with a heavy weight on top (a large plastic bottle of milk will do the job perfectly), taking care to regularly remove the water that the salmon releases.

4. When you are ready to serve, remove the dill and pepper from the salmon. The sugar and salt will have been absorbed by the fish; if any remains, you can wipe it off with paper towel.

5. Cut the salmon into thin slices and garnish with some fresh dill sprigs, thinly sliced lime, a drizzle of olive oil, and a few pink peppercorns. Your salmon is now ready to serve.

WHAT DOES GRAVLAX MEAN?

The Swedish word *gravlax* means "buried salmon" or "dried salmon." In the Middle Ages, there were no fridges, and so, to preserve fish, fishermen would salt and then bury it. This method was used not only for salmon but for all types of fish.

DAIRY PRODUCTS

Greek-style yogurt, lassi, or ayran: throughout the world, more than half a ton of yogurt is consumed every second. Which goes to show that we just can't get enough of this fermented dairy product, which has existed from time immemorial. Today, you can buy yogurt from the supermarket, but making it yourself allows you to rediscover all the subtleties of fermentation.

Lactic fermentation

Milk ferments as a result of two main bacteria: *Lactobacillus bulgaricus* and *Streptococcus thermophilus*, which feed on the sugar present in milk and produce lactic acid. This lactic acid destabilizes casein, the protein in cheese, which hardens. The result: yogurt and cheese.

YOGURT
WITHOUT A YOGURT-MAKER

It is all about temperature. Yogurt-making is easy and requires little equipment. The important thing is to respect the temperatures indicated, otherwise the enzymes will die and the yogurt won't take.

Equipment
- Glass pots with lids
- A kitchen thermometer

Ingredients
Makes 6 to 8 yogurts
- 4 ¼ cups (2 pints/1 liter) reduced-fat (semi-skimmed) milk
- A yogurt culture, or ½ pot of yogurt

1. In a saucepan, gently heat the milk. When it reaches 194°F (90°C), reduce the heat and let it simmer at between 176°F (80°C) and 194°F (90°C) for at least 20 minutes. The longer you simmer it, the thicker your yogurt will be. Let the milk cool gently until it reaches 131°F (55°C). If a skin forms on the surface, skim it off using a slotted spoon.

2. Tip the yogurt culture or half a pot of yogurt into a measuring jug. Pour in the equivalent of a glass of milk and stir. Pour this fermenting agent back into the milk and mix in well using a whisk.

3. Pour the liquid into the yogurt pots, seal with their lids, and place them somewhere warm. There are several options: on a radiator, in the sunshine, wrapped up in a blanket, in the oven at 131°F (55°C) (but turned off), in a cooking pot in a bain-marie. The aim is to reach the ideal temperature of 131°F (55°C).

4. After 3 hours, your yogurts should be done. If they are too liquid, let them ferment a while longer, checking them every hour. The longer you leave them in the heat, the firmer and sourer they will be.

The yogurts can be flavored with jam or fruit puree. Simply place 1 or 2 teaspoons in the bottom of each pot before you pour in the milk. You can also flavor the hot milk with vanilla or chocolate. For a sweetened yogurt, add some sugar or honey.

THE SALTED VERSION: LABNE

Typical of Syria and Lebanon, *labne* is eaten as an appetizer with bread. It is generally served with a drizzle of olive oil and sprinkled with za'atar, a spice mix containing thyme, oregano, sesame seeds, ground sumac, and other spices.

Equipment
- A sieve
- A piece of cheesecloth or a clean kitchen towel

Ingredients
- Your yogurts
- A pinch of salt

1. Add the salt to your yogurt and stir well.

2. Place a sieve over a mixing bowl and line with cheesecloth or a clean kitchen towel.

3. Pour in the yogurt, cover with cheesecloth or a kitchen towel, put a weight on top, and place the bowl in the fridge.

4. After 24 hours, your *labne* will be ready. If you want it to taste very fresh, you can eat it after 12 hours. Leave it longer if you want the cheese to be drier.

CHEESE

Cheese is made around the world, including in the United States, France, Japan, Italy, and, of course, Switzerland. As with wine, the starting point for all cheese is the terroir. Immerse yourself in the world of these delicious fermented dairy products.

THE FIGURE:

10. On average, you need to allow about 10 pints of milk to make 1 pound of cheese (or 10 liters per 1 kg). This makes sense, as cheese is composed mainly of milk from which water has been removed. Be aware that this figure varies a lot depending on the type of cheese you're making (and its size): for example, a camembert uses 3 ½ pints (2 liters), a Bleu d'Auvergne 42 pints (20 liters) and a wheel of Comté over 100 gallons (400 liters).

What happens when you make cheese?

1. To make cheese, the milk first has to be curdled. There are two ways of doing this: using lactic enzymes, as for yogurt, or rennet, which are enzymes of animal origin.

2. Once the milk has curdled, the milk is "cut" into small pieces. The larger the pieces are, the more water the cheese will contain.

3. The cheese is then drained and molded to help it drain. Hard cheeses are pressed to speed up this process, unlike soft cheeses, which retain more water.

4. Aging. The cheeses are stored in a cellar to gain in character. It is at this point that salt (for Emmental, for example), grape pomace (for Époisses), or mold (for Roquefort, for example) is added. The aging period varies significantly. Fresh goats' cheese is not aged at all, Roquefort is aged 3 months, Camembert 2 months and Comté 2 years. It all depends on the desired result. The longer the cheese is aged, the stronger it will taste.

Did you know that the first shop-bought yogurts were sold in pharmacies?
It was thanks to Isaac Carasso, a doctor from the Balkans who was practicing medicine in Barcelona, that the first industrial yogurts were sold in 1919—in pharmacies. Why? For their health benefits in treating digestive disorders, which many children were suffering from at that time. Subsequently, Carasso created his own yogurt production company, which he called Danone.

In what order should you eat cheeses from a cheese platter?

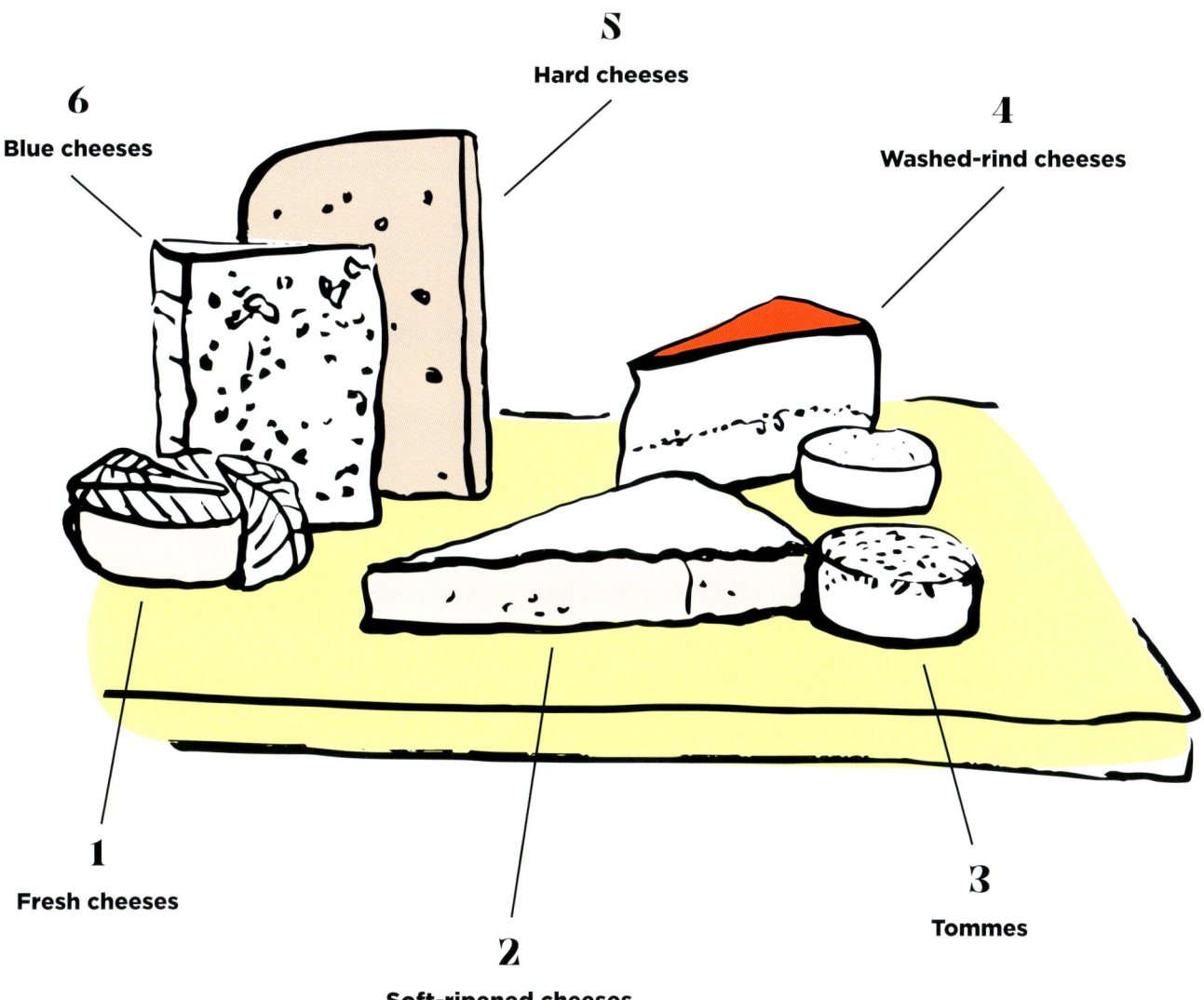

6 Blue cheeses
5 Hard cheeses
4 Washed-rind cheeses
3 Tommes
2 Soft-ripened cheeses
1 Fresh cheeses

Go by their age. The more mature a cheese is, the more it will tend to cover the taste of other cheeses.

PANCAKES, CREPES, AND BLINIS

Before bread there was the pancake! When you make pancakes today, you are probably unaware that they are the direct descendants of gruel, a dish widely consumed in the Neolithic era, some 4000 years BCE. You may likewise be unaware that pancakes, crepes, and blinis are also fermented foods. Luckily, everything is about to become clear!

The fermentation of pancakes

It is often said that in order to ensure that crepes or pancakes are light, you need to let the batter rest, in other words, let it ferment. Fermentation begins as soon as you mix flour with milk. Microorganisms begin to produce carbon dioxide, which makes the batter lighter, and the starch molecules are also predigested, making the pancakes more digestible. Ideally, you should let the batter rest overnight. This enables the microorganisms to get to work and gives the batter its flavor.

DOSA
INDIAN RICE AND LENTIL PANCAKES

These crepes, which are often stuffed with potatoes, chutney, or curry, are very popular throughout India. They are eaten at every meal, including breakfast. Easy to digest, they can make a complete meal that can be enjoyed by vegetarians, too.

Equipment
- 3 bowls
- A blender

Ingredients
Makes about 20 dosas
- ¾ cup (5 oz./150 g) sticky rice
- ¾ cup + 1 tbsp (5 oz./150 g) basmati rice
- ⅓ cup (2 ¼ oz./60 g) red or white lentils
- 1 tsp fenugreek seeds
- 1 tsp salt

1. Rinse the two types of rice separately, then place them in individual bowls. Cover with water and let soak for 6 hours. Do the same with the lentils.

2. After 6 hours, keeping each ingredient separate, drain the two types of rice and the lentils, blend them separately, then transfer everything to a large mixing bowl and stir together.

3. Add the fenugreek seeds and salt and stir using a wooden spoon.

4. Let ferment for 8 hours at room temperature. Make sure that your mixing bowl is big enough because the batter will take up a lot of space.

5. After 8 hours, your batter will be ready. If it feels too thick, add a little water so that it is easy to spread.

6. Cook the dosa as you would a crepe.

Dosas can be served with a vegetable or meat curry or with chutney, or can be used to add texture to a salad.

FERMENTED BUCKWHEAT CREPES

There are hundreds of recipes for buckwheat crepes. But the advantage of this one is that it contains neither eggs nor milk. It's therefore suitable for all types of diets. It is also left to rest 24 hours, which allows the batter to take on a range of flavors and makes it lighter.

Equipment
- A mixing bowl
- A pancake pan—or, better still, a Breton *billig* or crepe maker

Ingredients
Makes about 20 crepes
- 4 cups (1 lb. 2 oz./500 g) buckwheat flour
- 2 tsp salt
- 4 ½ cups (2 ½ pints/1.15 liters) warm water
- Fat for cooking

1. The day before, tip the flour and salt into a large mixing bowl, then gradually add most of the water (in about five lots), whisking continuously.

2. When the batter is smooth, drizzle the remaining water over the batter. It should form a protective barrier on the surface without penetrating it. Cover the bowl with a clean kitchen towel.

3. Let the batter rise for 24 hours in a cold room (or 12 hours if it is warm).

4. Whisk again so that the batter is completely smooth.

In Brittany (in the north of France), these pancakes are spread with salted butter. You can also fill them with ham, cheese, and an egg (known as the *complète* in Brittany), sausage and onions (*galette saucisse*), or for a sweet version, with salted butter caramel. Let your imagination run wild.

HOT SAUCES AND KETCHUP

Hot sauces and ketchup: when you think about these foods, you may find it hard to believe that you can make them at home—and that they're actually fermented. And yet, it is true! Now's your chance to discover these distinctive sauces.

Lactic fermentation

No surprises here, hot sauces like ketchup are made from vegetables, so it stands to reason that lactic fermentation comes into play in their production.
As a reminder, lactic fermentation functions with lactic bacteria, which feed on the sugar present in the vegetables and produce lactic acid. In the case of these sugars, all you have to do is ferment them in brine or feed them with different fermenting agents, such as Ginger Bug (see p. 147), lacto-fermented vegetable juice, or whey (the liquid that comes from fresh cheese when you strain it). These enzymes play the role of a fermenting agent: these liquids are actually full of microorganisms, which enable fermentation to begin.

KETCHUP

With its smooth texture, bittersweet flavor, and delicious tomato smell, ketchup is a taste of childhood. Originally, this sauce was fermented, even if you can no longer buy it in this form today. For this recipe, you can use either fresh tomatoes or good-quality canned ones.

Equipment
- A 10 ½ oz. (300 g) jar

Ingredients
For a 10 ½ oz. jar
- A fermenting agent: scant ½ cup (3 ½ fl. oz./100 ml) Ginger Bug (see p. 147) or whey
- 3 ¼ lb. (1.5 kg) fresh tomatoes or 1 ¾ lb. (800 g) canned peeled tomatoes
- 1 tbsp vinegar
- 1 tbsp soy sauce
- 1 tbsp honey
- ½ tsp salt
- Pinch of paprika
- Pinch of *quatre épices*
- ½ tbsp sugar, after fermentation

FROM *KE-TSIAP* TO KETCHUP: A WORLD OF FLAVORS

Ketchup comes from China, from where English sailors allegedly brought this spicy sauce, made with brine and fermented fish, home with them in their luggage. In England, mushrooms and onions were first added to the recipe, then tomatoes. It wasn't until 1876 that the American Henry John Heinz had the idea of adding sugar to it to create the ketchup we know today.

1. Wash and seed the tomatoes, then puree them in a blender. Strain them through a sieve, then place in a saucepan and boil for 3 minutes. The aim here is make filtering easier, not to cook the puree.

2. Place a sieve over a bowl and line it with a clean kitchen towel. Pour in the tomato puree and let stand for 12 hours. The tomato juice will drain.

3. After 12 hours, transfer the tomato juice into a mixing bowl and stir in all the other ingredients. The mixture should have the consistency of ketchup. If it is too thick, dilute it a little with some tomato juice until you have the desired consistency.

4. Fill the jar, leaving a ½ inch gap (1 cm) at the top. As with other lacto-fermented preserves, leave it at room temperature for 1 week, then store it in the fridge for at least 3 weeks. After this time, fermentation stops. Add a little sugar if the ketchup is too sour for your taste. Eat within a year.

Of course, when we think of ketchup, we think burgers or grilled meat. But you can also use it to make a meatloaf, puff-pastry cheese twists, or simply to add extra flavor to tomato juice.

Brewers' yeast for enhancing the taste of sauces

Brewers' yeast can usually be found in organic stores, in the form of flakes. Originally, this yeast was used to ferment beer. Today, it is known primarily for its nutritional benefits: it is very rich in vitamin B, which plays an important role in the vitality of nails and hair. What is less well known is that it can be added to sauces, soups, or stews—off the heat—to enhance their umami taste. It will make them tastier, as though they've been cooking for hours. Yet another of yeast's superpowers!

HOT SAUCE

From Thai sriracha to Argentinian chimichurri via Tunisian harissa, there are numerous recipes for hot sauces. Here is a basic one that you can adapt to your taste.

Equipment
- A 1-quart jar

Ingredients
- 9 oz. (250 g) chili peppers
- 1 onion
- 6 garlic cloves
- 1 oz. (30 g) fresh ginger
- 2 tbsp salt
- 4 ¼ cups (2 pints/1 liter) water
- 1 large cabbage leaf

THE CAROLINA REAPER: THE HOTTEST CHILI PEPPER IN THE WORLD

It comes from the United States and it is the hottest chili pepper in the world. It measures 1.6 million on the Scoville scale, which means it would need to be diluted 1.6 million times for its pungency to no longer be detectable. Note to lovers of very spicy food: you can buy it on the website of the company that markets it. Be warned, however, that you'll need a mask and gloves to handle it.

1. Wash the chili peppers and remove the stalks. If you want your sauce to be very hot, leave the seeds in; otherwise, remove and discard them. Cut the peppers into fairly thick slices, about 2 inches (5 cm) thick.

2. Peel the onion and the garlic cloves and quarter them. Peel the ginger and cut into large pieces. Put the chili peppers, garlic, onion, and ginger into a 2 pint (1 liter) sealable jar.

3. In a bowl, dissolve the salt in the water, then pour over the vegetables. Wedge the vegetables in place with the cabbage leaf. If necessary, add a weight to keep the vegetables submerged in the brine.

4. Let rest at room temperature for 7 days, then refrigerate for about 2 weeks.

5. After 2 weeks, you can blend the vegetables. Don't add all the brine straight away: add it gradually until the sauce is of the desired consistency. Consume within 6 months.

Added in small quantities to a dish, hot sauce acts as a flavor enhancer. In larger quantities, it will liven up a mayonnaise or a vegetable dish, for example.

THE CULTURAL IMPORTANCE OF BREAD

Whether it's jam on toast or a cream cheese bagel for breakfast, a pita filled with freshly made falafel for lunch, a thick slice of panettone with a cup of tea in the afternoon, or garlic croutons in an onion soup for supper, bread is one of the few foods that is eaten daily all around the world. Let's discover some of the main types.

BREAD: A REFLECTION OF OUR CULTURAL DIVERSITIES

Bread is eaten differently depending on whether you live in Australia, Argentina, the Ivory Coast, or Shanghai. It reflects our different cultures and is undoubtedly one of the foods that reveals the most about our eating habits.

In North Africa, it has a particularly important place: other dishes accompany it, but it is bread that is at the center of the table. In Singapore, people eat it for breakfast with *otha*, a fish puree. In the North of France, it is soaked in beer and cheddar: a dish known as *welsch*.

These examples illustrate the importance of bread in our cultures, wherever we live in the world.

The nine main families of bread

It is impossible to provide an exhaustive list of the all breads in the world. Nevertheless, based on their different characteristics, Lesaffre's bakers have managed to identify nine families of bread.

Crusty breads
These breads appeared in countries where wheat was grown. The art of baking developed in these places, helping to make crusty bread a traditional food, especially as the crust keeps the bread fresher longer. These breads include the French baguette, Italian ciabatta, and Austrian Kaiser roll. Industrialization and scientific progress during the nineteenth century (the appearance of refined flour, the mechanization of kneading, the commercialization of compressed yeast, etc.) largely contributed to transforming the traditional breadmaking process and led to the production of the crusty breads—of various shapes and using different ingredients—that we eat today. They can be produced from flour made from rye, barley, corn, or other grains, on their own or mixed with wheat flour. Today, the wide variety of such breads guarantees that there is something to satisfy everyone.

Sandwich bread
Common in the UK and the USA, it is also found in Mexico and Canada and in all the former British colonies in Asia and Australasia. American burger buns and Middle Eastern *kirpich* are part of this family. More surprisingly, in Japan, the soft milk bread *shokupan* represents more than 60 percent of total bread consumption.

Flatbreads
Flatbreads are among the most widely consumed breads in the world, whatever the continent. There are numerous varieties, including Lebanese bread, Egyptian *aish baladi*, Chinese *shaobing*, Sardinian *spianata*, pita, blini, injera, and, over the last few years, the wrap. Most of these come from around the Mediterranean.

Bread has a central place in these countries, rather than being served as an optional extra. It is accompanied with dates, figs, or a soup. It may also be stuffed with meat and with spices such as cumin, paprika, and coriander. Made from wheat flour or semolina, it can be savory or sweet, baked in the oven, on a baking sheet, in a tagine, or even directly over coals or on small hot stones, like the Iranian *sangak*.

Rye breads
Rye breads are traditionally consumed from Germany to Russia, like pumpernickel and Borodinsky. They are made with rye flour, which may be mixed with wheat flour, giving them their dark color. As these flours are very sticky, acidifiers such as sourdough starter, vinegar, or buttermilk are added to the dough. This is why these breads often have a sour taste. They have a long shelf life because they are very dense.

Fried breads
Fried breads are more like cereal gruels that have been fried than bread in the way that we think of it in the West. Examples are the Indian chapati, an unleavened bread that is fried in a skillet, the American donut, the German Berliner, and the Tanzanian *mandazi*.

Steamed breads
Originally from China, these very soft breads include Chinese *bao* and Central European *kluski*. In China, 20 percent of the wheat grown that is suitable for breadmaking is used in their manufacture. This type of bread is made from a dough prepared the day before that undergoes fermentation for two hours before it is cooked. On their own, they can seem a bit bland, but they are often stuffed with meat and/or vegetables and are served in dishes with a sauce.

Pizzas

Known by the same name worldwide, pizzas are the most commonly known type of bread on the planet. They are characterized by two key features: their round shape and their thickness—thin or thick depending on local preferences. In Naples, where pizza was invented in the sixteenth century, it takes the form of a galette spread with lard, cooked in a wood-fired oven, and served as a snack to bakery employees. The first pizza was therefore simply a white flatbread. It was only during the eighteenth century, when tomatoes imported from the Americas were no longer considered toxic, that Neapolitan bakers gave the pizza its red topping. Since then, pizza has continued to combine the most varied toppings, even including sweet ones.

Brioche doughs

Panettone, brioche, Latin American *concha*, and Asian *roti mani*: all these brioche-style breads have a high egg, fat, and sugar content. Their main characteristics? A soft crumb and a sweet taste that varies according to local tastes. These breads are consumed on every continent.

Puff pastries

From Greek *börek* to French croissants and *pains au chocolat*, puff pastries can be recognized by their numerous thin layers and their shiny golden crusts. They may be savory, like *börek*, or sweet, like *croissants*.

Two other categories complete this categorization: unfermented pastry products, such as American pancakes, and dry doughs, such as Italian grissini and rusks.

BREADS AROUND THE WORLD

Discovering the croissant

THE CROISSANT: SYMBOL OF FRENCH GASTRONOMY BUT OF VIENNESE ORIGIN

Contrary to popular belief, the croissant is not a French invention. It actually has quite a history.

Its origins date back to 1683, when the Austrian city of Vienna was being besieged by the Ottomans. To put an end to this long and costly occupation, the grand vizier decided to invade the city by digging an underground passage beneath its foundations. The tunnel's route passed by a bakery, whose workers heard suspicious noises. At first intrigued, and then anxious, they warned the Viennese guard, who sounded the alarm. Foiled in their plan, the Turks lifted the siege and left the city. The happy residents of Vienna decided to celebrate the occasion by creating a new pastry symbolizing the emblem of the Turkish flag: the crescent, or croissant. Originally made from a brioche-type dough, the croissant became popular throughout Austria.

Later, thanks to the presence of many Viennese bakers in Paris, the croissant was exported to France. It truly became popular, still in its brioche form, during the World's Fair in 1889. After the First World War, the croissant recipe changed to leavened and puffed dough, with alternating layers of dough and butter. So, the croissant as we know it today was invented in France, but its roots remain Viennese.

The croissant epitomizes enjoyable breakfast times the world over.

CHICAGO

"I am proud to be involved in promoting French bread!"

Déborah Libs, World-champion pastry chef,
Dinkel's Bakery Chicago

"I've participated in many competitions worldwide, which has helped me to increase my knowledge and to realize that there are no limits in creating new products. Today, I live in Chicago, where I run a French bakery. We work only with sourdough starter, to which we sometimes add yeast. You might imagine that Americans would not like these traditional flavors, but quite the opposite! The world of bread and pastries is exceptional and, like all good things, exports well!"

BREAD IN FIGURES

Humans first invented bread in Mesopotamia some 14,400 years ago.
10 billion baguettes are consumed every year throughout the world.
10 billion is also the number of living cells present in 1 gram of yeast.
The distance from the Earth to the moon: if all the cells in a 1 lb. 2 oz. (500 g) block of yeast were placed end to end, they would reach to the moon.
The three most consumed types of bread in the world:
- **crusty bread: 25%**
- **sandwich bread: 22%**
- **flatbreads: 21%**

Bread: a mine of nutrients

Bread has an important place in most cultures. And it is easy to understand why. What a pleasure it is to bite into a slice of fresh bread. Did you know, for example, that it contains more than 540 aromatic molecules? It has wheaty, nutty, and yeasty notes, of course, but bread is also a mine of nutrients. Let's explore this very complete food.

A very important part of our diet

There are numerous vitamins in bread, including B1, B2, PP, and E. Vitamins B1, B2, and PP are the ones that help us think, while vitamin E has antioxidant properties. The vitamins in bread come from the wheat germs and outer husks, which is why their amount varies depending on the type of flour used. White bread, made from white flour, contains six times fewer vitamins than brown bread.

Bread is also an important source of protein (including amino acids and peptides) that contribute to the renewal of our cells. It contains 7 to 8 percent of low-fat vegetable proteins and as such is excellent for muscle tissue. When we eat bread for breakfast, we avoid a mid-morning low, thanks to the starch—those famous slow-burning carbs—it contains. They enable us to regulate our feelings of hunger without adding lots of sugar and fat.

What is less well known is that whole wheat flour is also a good source of minerals, including magnesium, potassium, and phosphorus, which enable our body and mind to function well. But beware: bread made with white flour contains very few. The choice is yours.

WHERE DO RUSKS COME FROM?

Rusks were invented in the fifteenth century by sailors who made long sea voyages. They brought along flat breads that had been cooked twice to remove all traces of moisture, which prevented them from going stale. The *bis-cuit* (meaning cooked twice) was born. Much later, in 1903, Charles Heudebert, a French baker, invented the *biscotte* by baking first sandwich-style bread then its individual slices. He decided to call it *biscotte*, from the Italian word for biscuit: *biscotto*.

THE INGREDIENTS IN BREAD

Flour

The main ingredient in bread, flour is obtained by finely milling cereal grains such as wheat, buckwheat, or corn. This process is necessary to remove the outer shell (the bran), which is made of cellulose and which we cannot digest, from the wheat kernel.

Different flour, different bread

Each country has its own way of classifying flour, sometimes based on the bran content, sometimes on the protein content, and occasionally on both.
Millers offer a wide range of different flours, from white to wholemeal, that vary according to the type of cereal and how finely it is ground. Whole wheat flour contains a significant amount of bran and, as the majority of vitamins, minerals, and fiber are found in the bran, it also contains the most nutrients.

Water

This is the link between the bread's different ingredients, without which fermentation cannot begin. Tap water is fine for making bread. If your water is too chlorinated, let it rest for 1 to 2 hours before use.

Salt

Salt is an essential ingredient in breadmaking. It enhances flavors, slows down fermentation, and firms up the dough and makes it more elastic. It also has antioxidant properties. The World Health Organization nevertheless recommends reducing the amount of salt in food. For recommended quantities, refer to the recipes at the end of this section (see pp. 102–114).

PIZZA IS ALSO BREAD!

30 billion: the number of pizzas consumed worldwide. Americans are the biggest pizza eaters in the world, consuming 28 1/2 lb. (13 kg)/year/person, way ahead of the French (17 1/2 lb./8 kg), the Italians (11 lb./5 kg), and the Germans (9 lb./4 kg).

Fermenting agents

No yeast, no bread…

Whatever the breadmaking process, the baker cannot do without yeast because it is the essential ingredient for fermentation. Of course, the primary function of yeast is to enable the dough to rise, but it also helps develop flavor. The best-known yeast, *Saccharomyces cerevisiae*, excels in this role. These microscopic fungi feed on the glucose and fructose contained in flour, enabling fermentation to take place. During this transformation, the yeasts produce carbon dioxide, which is trapped in the cells of the crumb.

Some yeasts also have other powers. *Chevalieri*, for example, has great fermentation ability. Bakers use it, notably to tone down certain sourdough notes, such as the sour taste. It acts as a flavor enhancer and accentuates the nutty flavor resulting from fermentation.

Bacteria: allies of yeasts

In a sourdough starter, yeasts and bacteria coexist in symbiosis. To date, more than twenty-five species of yeasts and more than fifty bacteria species have been identified in breadmaking leavens throughout the world. Bacteria help with fermentation and complete the bread's aromatic profile. In particular, they develop the acidity typical of sourdough—acetic, lactic, or fruity—as well as other aromatic notes, depending on the recipes.

Baker's yeast: a revolution in the world of bread

In 1872, the first yeast factory was established at Maisons-Alfort, a suburb of Paris. It was headed up by Baron Max von Springer, who revolutionized the world of baking. His yeast, produced on a large scale with controlled processes, enabled bakers to obtain greater regularity in their production and to offer a high quality product to a greater number of people. Sourdough, on the other hand, is a much more complex substance in terms of its composition. It is also very sensitive to temperature changes and to external contaminants. It requires a lot of experience to cultivate starters and exploit their full potential in breadmaking.

DID YOU KNOW?

In order to reduce the sugar and fat content of some bakery products (brioche, for example), you can add vanilla, which compensates for these reductions (up to 30 percent of sugar) and reveals buttery and round notes on the palate. Natural vanillin is obtained by the bioconversion of ferulic acid present in the husks of certain corn and rice kernels. The result: a natural and vegetal aroma that adds a touch of vanilla to brioche and other pastries. This aroma is even more interesting in that it also gives the sensation of sugar and fat. The result: a vanilla-flavored brioche with a lower fat and sugar content.

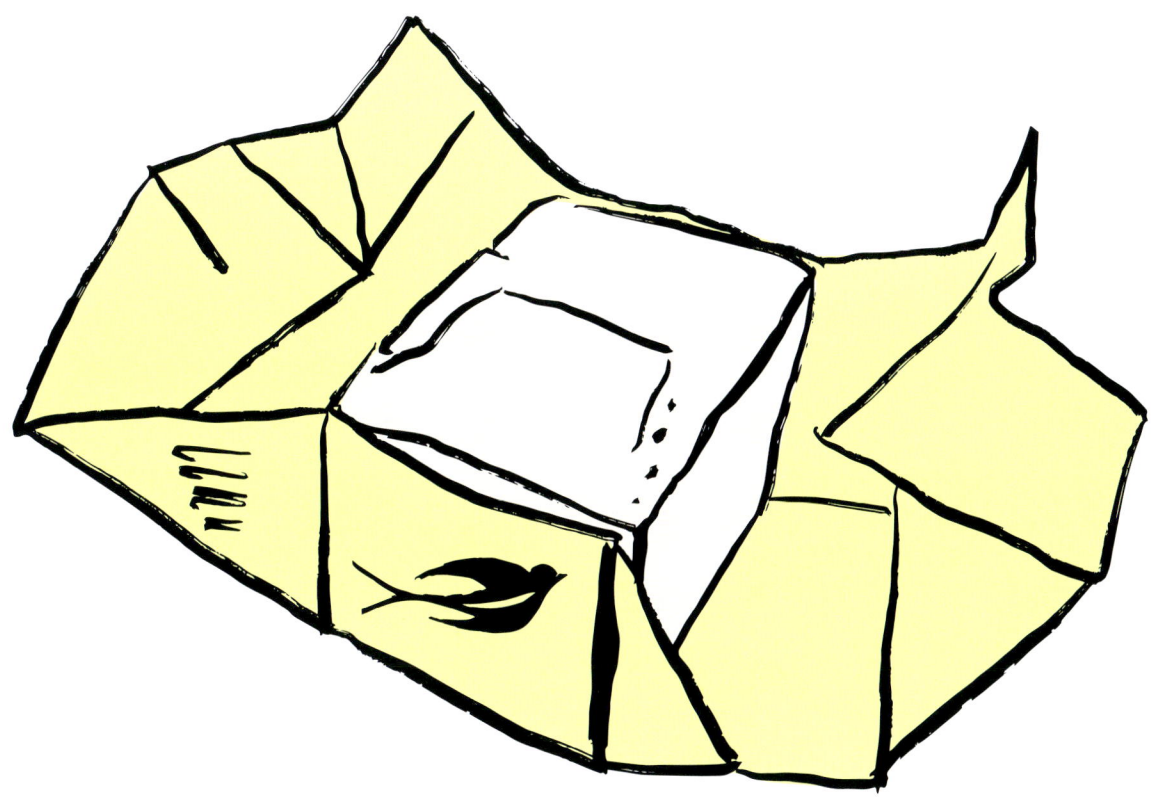

"Yeasts and sourdough starters: the magic of fermentation!"

Joël Defives - Meilleur Ouvrier de France (Best craftsman of France)

"When I began as a baker, in the early 1980s, nobody was making sourdough, only bread made with commercial yeast. Several generations of bakers didn't even know how to use it. I was lucky because my apprenticeship supervisor taught me this method. He showed me the trick of adding a dose of yeast at the beginning of kneading sourdough, so I've always made bread with a combination of sourdough and yeast. In limited quantities, they enable us to boost fermentation and make it more stable. And that's a real advantage for bakers as well as consumers. Today, in general, we master our trade better, with fermentation, richer flours, methodical kneading, and bakeries equipped with fridges. The bread we eat has never tasted so good or been better for us."

How is baker's yeast made?

Before arriving at the bakery, certain yeasts are first of all selected for their fermenting abilities. They are then placed in a favorable atmosphere, where they duplicate by budding many times. By the thirty-fourth budding, a single cell will have produced seventeen billion more. They are then separated from their culture medium by centrifugation, then dehydrated. This is why there are several billion identical cells in a cube of baker's yeast.

BAKING POWDER AND BAKER'S YEAST: TWO VERY DIFFERENT THINGS

Baker's yeast is a living organism. Baking powder is an additive composed of sodium bicarbonate, an acidic agent, and a neutral agent like starch. It is used only in baking and has no fermentation ability. To cause the dough to rise, it employs a simple chemical reaction, but there is no fermentation. Dough therefore needs to be cooked soon after the baking powder is added or it risks collapsing. Fermented dough, on the other hand, can continue to rise for several hours. Baker's yeast is used for bread, brioches, croissants, and pizza. Some cakes, such as rum baba, are also made using baker's yeast.

Sourdough

Throughout the world, there are hundreds of names for sourdough: it all depends on which of its features are focused on. Sometimes, it is about its ability to make dough rise, notably thanks to yeasts, such as the French word "levain," which comes from the Latin *levare*, meaning to rise, or the term *massa levedura* in Portuguese. For others, the sour aspect, relating to the bacteria, is emphasized, as in the English word "sourdough" or the German *sauerteig*.

Sourdough is the result of a mixture of water and flour that has undergone fermentation due to the combined effect of yeasts and bacteria naturally present in nature. Sourdough fermentation generates lactic and acetic acids, which play a large part in the flavor (the sensation provoked by both taste and smell) of the final product, and the levels of which depend on the fermentation conditions.

In fact, the art of mastering sourdough lies in understanding and managing the balance created within it. The taste that sourdough gives bread depends on the synergy between microorganisms, their development conditions (temperature, hydration, fermentation time, frequency of nutrient inputs), and the type of grain used. This requires great precision and expertise. Rye adds a slightly fruity taste of cooked prunes; barley and oats add a spicy note to the sourdough. Durum wheat softens the flavor on the palate, giving it a buttery and milky taste, like pancake batter. Buckwheat gives it a powerful taste of hay and cut grass that can be found in specialty breads.

Bakers who make their own sourdough starter need to maintain it, refresh it, and make it grow daily. It needs to be fed (with water and flour) by vigorously mixing the dough. If you forget it, it will die. Some bakers therefore make it a habit to never go on vaca-

tion without their starter, or they entrust the task of maintaining and refreshing it to an employee during their absence. In general, sourdough keeps better than yeast bread because it is denser and more acidic. Acidity is a natural preservative because it inhibits the development of mold; moisture escapes less easily. It is also less crusty.

Over recent years, sourdough breads have become popular again with consumers around the world in search of natural qualities and tradition.

GINGER STARTER ALSO EXISTS

The word "starter" is often used in the context of baking. What is less known is that a starter is a generic term, referring to a mixture of microorganisms that serve to activate fermentation. So, we speak of ginger starter (water, ginger, and sugar) to make ginger beer (see p. 148), apple starter to make cider, and even potato starter to make bread.

THE FERMENTATION OF BREAD

In the absence of oxygen in the dough, yeasts convert the glucose into carbon dioxide and metabolites, including organic acids. Fermentation thus releases nutrients trapped within the cellular structures of grains of wheat, for example.

This is particularly the case with whole wheat bread, which is popular with nutritionists because of its high nutritional value. It is richer in nutrients and minerals because it contains the whole grain, including the bran and the germ that it surrounds. But fermentation is vital: if this isn't sufficient, your body will not be able to assimilate the minerals and nutrients that remain in (wheat or rye) whole wheat breads. Under-fermented, this type of bread can even have a decalcifying effect.

BREAD LIKES A GOOD ATMOSPHERE

To ensure even fermentation, the temperature needs to remain moderate, between 68 and 86°F (20–30°C). This will enable the yeasts to do their work with ease. The same is true of the humidity level of the room. If the air is too dry, the dough will tend to dry out and may split. Too humid, and it will become sticky and difficult to work with.

The main stages of breadmaking

1. Kneading. This is when all the ingredients are mixed together and kneaded. The aim here is to hydrate the ingredients and to develop the gluten structure in the dough, in other words to establish the balance between elasticity and extensibility that will enable the bread to retain the gas created by the fermentation process and the baker to shape the dough as they wish.

2. Bulk fermentation. The first rise—the first stage of fermentation—takes place before the dough is divided into pieces. It continues the action started previously and gives body to the dough. The longer the dough is left to rise, the more it will gain in strength. It is also at this stage that fermentation develops all its aromas.

3. Shaping. Giving the bread its final shape, which should allow the gas created by fermentation to be retained.

4. Final proofing. This is the final fermentation stage. The dough pieces rise, and may double or even triple in size. But beware, proofing should not last too long or the dough may collapse.

5. Scoring. The surface of the dough is cut with a sharp blade to help it develop well. Water vapor and carbon dioxide will escape through these cuts while the bread is baking. This is also a way in which the baker can "sign" their bread.

6. Baking The dough continues to rise at the start of baking, but the yeasts very quickly die off when the temperature reaches 131°F (55°C). Between 158 and 176°F (70–80°C), the proteins (gluten) coagulate and the starch gelatinizes. The air sacs develop in the crumb. The crust begins to brown at around 340°F (170°C) (the Maillard reaction and caramelization) and to solidify at around 390°F (200°C). As the baker puts the bread in the oven, they blast a jet of steam into the oven. This prevents the dough from drying out too quickly and allows the crust to take its time to form. It also smooths out any lumps on the surface, which will make the bread shinier and help it brown well.

7. Cooling This is the necessary resting time for bread. This is why, when you buy a baguette that is still hot, it is best to leave the paper bag open. Otherwise, the crust will soon lose its crispness.

THE MAILLARD REACTION

This concerns not only bread, but any foods that are baked. The proteins contained in the food interact with the residual sugar and form a brown layer that, in bread, is the crust.

Storing bread

There are many ways to keep bread fresh, but there are no magic formulas. To keep it as long as possible, choose an open-crumb bread, which is typical of sourdough. The openness of the cells will slow down the migration of water from the crumb and the drying out of the bread. To keep it a few days, you can wrap it in a clean kitchen towel once it has cooled. When it is beginning to get a little dry, sprinkle it with water and then heat it a few minutes in the oven at 210°F (100°C/Gas mark 1/4). This method is surprisingly effective.

Finally, you can freeze your bread, preferably sliced, so that you can defrost only the slices you need. Once defrosted, bread will go stale very quickly—in a matter of a few hours.

Baking bread at home

Bakers' tips

- Weigh all the ingredients.
- Dust your work counter with flour, but not too much, or you will add too much flour to your dough and this will create coarse folds in the crumb.
- To reproduce the baking conditions of a professional oven, place a thick tile or stone on the oven rack and bake your bread directly on it. It will radiate heat more evenly.
- Find your own recipe. Homemade bread deserves your attention and it is worth finding the recipe that suits you.

You are now ready to go! Here are our recipes to get you started.

SIX EASY RECIPES

MULTI-GRAIN BREAD

Makes 1 loaf

Prep time: 15 minutes
Resting time: 4 hours + overnight for the grains
Baking time: 40 minutes

Ingredients

- 1 ⅓ cup (7 oz./200 g) mixed seeds (sesame, flax, millet, poppy, buckwheat, etc.)
- 1 cup (½ pint/250 ml) water + scant ½ cup for soaking the seeds
- 3 ¾ cups (1 lb. 2 oz./500 g) bread flour
- ⅓ cup (3 1/2 oz./100 g) refreshed sourdough starter
- 1 tsp (3 g) fresh baker's yeast
- 1 ¾ tsp (9 g) salt

HOW DO YOU KNOW IF THE BREAD IS BAKED?

When you tap with your fingertips on the flat part (the bottom) of the loaf, it should make a hollow sound.

1. The day before, prepare the seeds. Preheat the oven to 400°F (200°C/Gas mark 6). Spread the seeds out on a baking sheet and roast for 10 minutes. Heat a scant ½ cup (3 ½ fl. oz./100 ml) of water until it boils. Place half the seeds in a bowl and cover them with the boiling water. Let cool, then cover the bowl. Refrigerate overnight so that the seeds absorb the water.

2. The following day, drain if necessary. In the bowl of a food processor fitted with the dough hook, place 1 cup (½ pint/250 ml) of water, the flour, sourdough, crumbled yeast, and salt. Knead 3 minutes on low speed, then 4 to 6 minutes on medium speed. Once kneaded, stir in half the soaked seeds.

3. Shape the dough into a ball, cover, and let rise for 1 to 2 hours in a warm place. After 30 minutes, fold the dough, then fold again after an hour.

4. When the dough has risen, place it on a flour-dusted work counter and quickly shape it into a ball. Cover it with a clean kitchen towel and rest for 15 minutes.

5. Shape the bread into a ball and place it in a banneton (proofing basket), seam side up. Cover with a clean kitchen towel or a large container and let stand for 2 hours.

6. Preheat the oven to 500°F (260°C/Gas mark 9) and place a bread stone, or failing that a baking tray, inside it, with a drip tray underneath.

7. When the loaf has risen well, turn it onto a peel. Brush it with a little water, then sprinkle with the remaining seeds. Score the loaf and put it in the oven quickly, then pour a bowl of hot water into the drip tray. Quickly close the oven door.

8. Bake in the oven for 20 minutes. After 20 minutes, lower the oven temperature to 425°F (220°C/Gas mark 7) and continue baking for 20 minutes.

9. When the top is golden brown and the underside sounds hollow when tapped, take the bread out of the oven and let it cool on a wire rack.

BAGUETTE

Makes 4 small (10 in./25 cm) baguettes

Prep time: 15 minutes
Resting time: 3 hours + 1h30 + 15 hours + 30 minutes + 30 minutes
Baking time: 18 minutes

Ingredients

- 3 ¾ cups (1 lb. 2 oz./500 g) bread flour
- 1 ½ cups (12 fl. oz./350 ml) water
- Scant ¼ cup (2 oz./50 g) refreshed sourdough starter
- ⅓ tsp (1 g) fresh baker's yeast
- ½ tbsp (7 g) salt

1. Pour the flour and water into the bowl of a food processor fitted with the dough hook. Mix for 1 minute on low speed. Cover and rest for 3 hours. Add the sourdough starter and crumbled yeast to the dough. Dissolve the salt in 2 teaspoons of water, then add to the dough. Knead for 8 minutes on low speed.

2. Cover the bowl and let the dough rest for 1h30, folding it every 30 minutes. Let rise for 15 hours in the fridge.

3. Dust the work counter and the dough with flour. Turn the dough out, with the non-floured surface toward you. Divide the dough into four pieces and form them into long strips. Rest for 30 minutes at room temperature.

4. Shape the baguettes and lay them in a lightly floured clean kitchen towel, folded concertina-style, so that the baguettes don't touch each other. Be careful to ensure that you shape your baguettes to fit your oven (they will be easier to place in the oven if they are shorter). Rest for 20 minutes.

5. Preheat the oven to 500°F (260°C/Gas mark 9) and place a bread stone, or failing that a baking tray, inside it, with a drip tray underneath. Using a board, place the baguettes onto the hot stone or baking sheet. Score the tops of the baguettes. Pour a bowl of hot water into the drip tray. Bake for 18 minutes, reducing the oven temperature to 475°F (240°C) halfway through the cooking time, then transfer the baguettes to a wire rack to cool.

SIX EASY RECIPES

PRETZELS

Makes 8 pretzels

Prep time: 35 minutes
Resting time: 10 minutes + 1h30
Baking time: 18 to 23 minutes

Ingredients

For the pretzels
- ½ cup + 2 tbsp
  (5 fl. oz./150 ml) water
- ½ cup + 2 tbsp
  (5 fl. oz./150 ml) milk
- 1 packet active dry yeast
- 4 cups (1 lb. 2 oz./500 g)
  all-purpose flour
- 2 tsp salt
- 2 ¾ tbsp (1 ½ oz./40 g) semi-salted
  butter, at room temperature
- 1 egg yolk
- Fleur de sel

For the cooking water
- 4 ¼ cups (2 pints/1 liter) water
- 2 tsp salt
- ¼ cup (2 oz./55 g) baking soda

1. Warm the water and milk, then stir in the yeast and let rest for 10 minutes. Pour the water into the bowl of a food processor and add the flour, the water/milk/yeast mixture, and the butter. Knead the dough 5 to 7 minutes on low speed, then cover the bowl and let the dough rise for about 1h30. The dough should double in volume.

2. Preheat the oven to 400°F (200°C/Gas mark 6). Divide the dough into eight pieces. Roll each piece of dough into a sausage, then shape into a pretzel. In a large saucepan, heat the water with the salt and baking soda. Plunge each pretzel into the boiling liquid for about 3 minutes, then lay them onto a baking sheet covered with parchment paper.

3. In a small bowl, whisk the egg yolk with a little water. Brush the pretzels with the beaten egg, then sprinkle them with the fleur de sel. Bake in the oven for 15 to 20 minutes, until golden. Let cool on a wire rack.

GUA BAOS

Makes 6 *gua baos*

Prep time: 30 minutes
Resting time: 1h30 to 2h + 20 minutes + 1 hour
Cooking time: 10 minutes + 40 minutes

Ingredients

For the *gua baos*
- 2 ⅓ cups (10 ½ oz./300 g) all-purpose flour
- 5 level tsp (¾ oz./20 g) sugar
- 1 tsp active dry yeast
- 1 tsp baking powder
- ¼ tsp salt
- ½ cup + 2 tbsp (5 fl. oz./150 ml) reduced-fat milk

For the filling
- 10 ½ oz. (300 g) pork belly
- 1 tbsp oil
- 2 garlic cloves, finely chopped
- 1 tbsp cane sugar
- 1 tbsp grated fresh ginger
- 1 tsp five-spice powder
- ½ tsp ground cinnamon
- 1 star anise
- Scant ½ cup (3 1/2 fl. oz./100 ml) rice vinegar
- Scant ½ cup (3 1/2 fl. oz./100 ml) soy sauce
- Scant ½ cup (3 1/2 fl. oz./100 ml) water

To serve
- Kimchi (see recipe on p. 52) or crudités
- A few cilantro leaves
- 2 tbsp roasted salted peanuts, roughly chopped

For the *gua baos*

1. Pour the flour, sugar, yeast, baking powder, salt, and milk into the bowl of a food processor fitted with the dough hook. Knead for 5 to 6 minutes on low-to-medium speed, until you have a very supple dough. Cover the bowl and let the dough rise for 1h30 to 2 hours.

2. Turn the dough out onto a flour-dusted work counter. Using a dough cutter, divide the dough into six equal pieces and roughly shape into balls. Cover and let rest for 20 minutes.
Cut twelve squares of parchment paper, each 4 inches (10 cm) square. Using a rolling pin, roll each dough ball into a 6 x 3-inch (16 x 8-cm) oval. Place a square of parchment paper over one half of each dough oval and fold over the other half. Lay these *gua bao* on another square of parchment paper.

3. Place the *gua baos* and their papers into a steam-cooker basket and let for rise 1 hour. Steam cook the *gua baos* for 10 minutes on a low heat so that they don't split.

For the filling

Trim the pork belly and cut into 1/2-inch (1-cm) thick slices. In a cooking pot, brown the pork slices in the oil, then add the other filling ingredients. Cover the pan and let simmer for about 40 minutes. Add more water if necessary. The meat should be tender and caramelized.

To serve

Fill each *gua bao* with a slice of caramelized pork, a little kimchi or a few crudités, a few cilantro leaves, and some chopped peanuts.

PITAS

Makes 10 pitas

Prep time: 15 minutes
Resting time: 20 minutes + 2 hours + 30 minutes to 1 hour + 10 minutes
Cooking time: 30 minutes

Ingredients

- 1 packet active dry yeast
- 1 ½ cups (12 fl. oz./350 ml) water
- 4 cups (1 lb. 2 oz./500 g) all-purpose flour
- 5 level tsp (¾ oz./20 g) sugar
- 1 ¾ tsp (9 g) salt
- 1 ½ tbsp olive oil

1. In the bowl of a food processor fitted with the dough hook, mix the yeast with the water. Add half the flour and all the sugar and knead for 2 minutes on low speed, just to combine the ingredients. Let rest for 20 minutes. Add the remainder of the flour and the salt. Knead 3 minutes on low speed, then 5 to 7 minutes on medium speed. Add the oil 3 minutes before the end of kneading.

2. Cover the bowl and let the dough rise for 2 hours in a warm place, folding it twice during this fermentation time.

3. Place the dough onto a flour-dusted work counter and shape into ten balls, each weighing 3 ½ oz. (100 g). Cover with a clean, damp kitchen towel and let rest for 30 minutes to 1 hour.

4. Using a rolling pin or your hands, roll out or flatten the dough balls to $^{1}/_{16}$ to ¼-inch (2 to 5 mm) thick. Let them rest on a flour-dusted baking sheet or board, uncovered, for 10 minutes.

5. Heat a heavy-based non-stick skillet. Place a pita in it and let it rise slightly. Turn it over and let it rise completely. Repeat to cook the remaining pitas.

6. Wrap the pitas in a clean kitchen towel or place them in a plastic bag so that they remain soft until you are ready to fill them.

SIX EASY RECIPES

FOCACCIA

Makes 1 focaccia

Prep time: 20 minutes
Resting time: 20 to 30 minutes
+ 3 hours + 20 minutes + 2 hours
Baking time: 30 minutes

Ingredients

For the focaccia
- 2 ¾ cups (12 oz./350 g) all-purpose flour
- 1 ¼ cups (10 ½ oz./300 g) water
- ⅓ cup (3 ½ oz./100 g) refreshed sourdough starter
- ½ tbsp (5 g) fresh baker's yeast
- ½ tbsp salt diluted in 1 tbsp water
- 1 tbsp olive oil + extra for the baking sheet
- Fleur de sel

For the topping
- Cherry tomatoes, halved, olives, rosemary

1. Pour the water into the bowl of a food processor and add the sourdough starter, crumbled yeast, and flour. Mix for 2 minutes on low speed. Cover the bowl and let rest for 20 to 30 minutes.

2. Mix on low speed for 4 to 6 minutes. With the food processor still running, add the salt and drizzle in the oil. Increase the speed to medium and knead for 5 to 7 minutes.

3. Cover the bowl (the dough will be quite soft and runny, but that is normal), and let rise for 3 hours in a warm place, folding it every 30 minutes.

4. Generously oil a high-sided baking sheet. Oil your hands, then spread the dough out, without tearing it, to cover the baking sheet. If it is difficult to spread, let rest for 20 minutes.

5. Press the entire surface of the dough with your fingertips. Sprinkle with olive oil and let rise for 2 hours. After 1 hour, press the dough again with your fingertips.

6. Preheat the oven to 450°F (230°C/Gas mark 8) and place the shelf in the middle of the oven with a drip tray underneath. Cover the dough with the halved cherry tomatoes, olives, and rosemary. Put the focaccia into the oven, quickly pour a bowl of hot water into the drip pan, and close the oven door. Bake for 30 minutes. Slide the focaccia out onto a wire rack, sprinkle with fleur de sel, and let cool.

GOOD TO KNOW

Do not use extra-virgin olive oil to oil the baking sheet. Keep it for seasoning the focaccia when you remove it from the oven. Use regular olive oil, which has a higher smoke point (the temperature at which it begins to burn).

You can also make yeast-only focaccia. In this case, omit the sourdough starter and use ⅓ oz. (10 g) of fresh yeast.

XAVIER HONORIN'S ROLLS

Partner of the Tour de France and world bakery champion

Ingredients

For 2 ¼ lb. (1 kg) dough, which makes 25 mini rolls (1 oz./25 g each) or 5 hamburger buns (3 ½ oz./100 g each)

- 4 cups (1 lb. 2 oz./520 g) all-purpose flour
- Scant ¼ cup (1 ½ oz./40 g) sugar
- 2 tsp salt
- ⅓ oz (10 g) fresh baker's yeast
- ⅓ cup + 2 tbsp (3 ½ oz./100 g) butter
- 1 cup (7 ½ oz./220 ml) water
- Scant ¼ cup (1 ¾ fl. oz /50 ml) milk
- 1 egg

Toppings

With the Espelette pepper
- some red quinoa

With the curry powder
- toasted flaked almonds

With the pesto
- Parmesan shavings

With the walnuts
- pieces of crushed walnut

1. Use fresh tap water and milk and an egg straight from the fridge.

2. In a food processor fitted with the whisk attachment, mix all the ingredients for 3 minutes on low speed then 6 minutes on medium speed.

3. After mixing, you can customize your rolls by adding the following ingredients to the dough:
- 2 tsp Espelette pepper + 1 tbsp paprika
- 2 ½ tsp curry powder
- Generous ¼ cup (2 ½ oz./70 g) pesto + 2 ½ tbsp all-purpose flour
- ⅔ cup (2 oz./55 g) ground walnuts + 2 tbsp walnut oil

4. Let the dough rest for 30 minutes at room temperature then 30 minutes in the fridge.

5. Divide the dough into 1 oz. (25 g) pieces.

6. Let rest for 10 minutes, then flatten lightly using your hand or a rolling pin.

7. Cover with a damp, clean kitchen towel and let ferment, in a draft-free place, for 1 hour to 1 hour 30 minutes.

8. Using a pastry brush, gently brush the surface of the rolls with beaten egg, then sprinkle with toppings, depending on the flavoring used in the dough.

9. Bake in the oven, preheated to 325°F (160°C/Gas mark 3), for 8 minutes.

"When baking, whether at home or elsewhere, you have to know how to indulge yourself!" Xavier Honorin

"When baking, at home or elsewhere, you have to know how to indulge yourself—with soft white bread, for example, which you can enjoy at any time of day, savory or sweet. Spread with jam for breakfast, as a toasted sandwich for lunch, for canapés with pre-dinner drinks, or even in bread-and-butter pudding—anything's possible. And you can use the same dough to make hamburger buns or rolls, like the ones in this recipe. There's no end to the possibilities. That's what I love about my job: trying out new ideas, launching new products! Being a baker today is nothing like it was in the past, and that's what makes it so interesting!"

FERMENTED DRINKS: ELIXIRS FULL OF ORIGINALITY

Fermented drinks have existed for thousands of years. Milk kefir, for example, dates back to 3500 BCE. But over the years, they were forgotten. Fortunately, we now have the pleasure of rediscovering these drinks full of health benefits. Enter this world and discover an endless field of possibilities. You can prepare delicious-tasting drinks with all kinds of flavors using bacteria and yeast.

Beer, wine, cider, and liquors—all fermented drinks—are often enjoyed with family and friends. And this has been the case since time immemorial. Did you know, for example, that during the time of the pharaohs, workers were paid in beer? The story has it that they could receive up to five pints of beer a day. All the more reason to be impressed at the colossal achievement of the pyramids!

In this chapter, we are going to discover the secrets of the main alcoholic and non-alcoholic fermented drinks. Because fermentation does not necessarily mean alcoholization.

BEER
The ancient story of beer

Judging by clay tablets showing an example of drinks made from fermented grains, it seems that Sumerians were already making beer some eight thousand years ago. In Egypt, in 2650 BCE, beer was consumed more than water, which often carried diseases. Alcoholic fermentation killed pathogenic bacteria, and beer was consumed by everyone, even children. But it was not until the Middle Ages that its manufacture and trade really took off, particularly in abbeys and monasteries.

Today, many of us still enjoy beer. In 2020, more than 50 billion gallons were produced worldwide. Indeed, over the past few years, the sector has been booming. Fermentation techniques, the selection of raw ingredients, blends, and new breweries have pushed back boundaries, much to our delight.

BEER IN FIGURES

39 gallons (148 liters): the annual beer consumption per capita by Czechs—a world record. By way of comparison, US consumption is 28.2 gallons (106.7 liters) per capita (adults aged 21 and over).
9,000: the number of breweries in the US in 2020.
What you will find in 9 fl. oz. (250 ml) of beer:
12 fl. oz. (350 ml) water, 2 oz. (50 g) malt,
1/16 oz. (2 g) hops, a pinch of yeast.
It takes three gallons of water to brew one gallon of beer in modern breweries. And this quantity can increase to fifty gallons.

What is beer made of?

The main ingredient in beer is water. This is why brewers attach great importance to it. Some of its mineral salts, such as iron, magnesium, and calcium, can even affect the longevity of the head (the frothy foam on the top of the beer).

The other ingredients needed to produce beer are malt, hops, and yeast. Hops contribute mainly to the microbiological stability of the must and to the organoleptic characteristics (taste, flavor, and smell) finished product's. Hops belong to the *Cannabaceae* family, the most well-known member of which is cannabis. Malt is a germinated cereal grain (barley, wheat, oats) that constitutes the main source of the sugars needed for fermentation and contributes significantly to the beer's consistency and color.

There are two main families of beer: lagers, which are cool fermented, contain fewer esters (aromatic molecules resulting from the condensation of alcohol with other components), and are very thirst-quenching; and ales, which are warm fermented, are typically characterized by more flavor and aromatic complexity, and contain more alcohol.

How is beer made?

1. Malting. This process takes place in the malt house, where the grains of barley, wheat, or other grains are germinated by soaking them in water under specific temperature conditions. The aim of the process is to produce the enzymes needed to break down the starch molecules (energy stores needed for the grain to grow) during brewing. The final stage in malting consists in stopping the germination process and drying—kilning—the grain. This process also enables the grain to develop its color, which will characterize that of the finished beer. Pale, caramelized, and roasted malts can thus be distinguished.

2. Mashing. The malt produced in the malt house and delivered to the brewery is crushed to expose the starch to the surrounding environment. The flour—grist—thus produced is mixed with water to create a dough that will be transformed as the temperature is raised in successive stages, each stage allowing a specific enzyme to break down the starch, either into simple fermentable sugars or into complex sugars, which will contribute to the body of the beer. This stage consists in producing a sugar syrup that is known as "wort."

3. Boiling. This wort is then boiled. During this stage, the first hops are added; a first quantity at the start of boiling, which gives beer its bitter character, and a second at the end of the boiling process, which contributes to its aromatic character. Various spices may also be added at this stage. Boiling also sterilizes the wort and eliminates undesirable elements such as the beginnings of flawed tastes and factors that could cause the beer to be unstable.

4. Fermentation. At the end of the boiling stage, the wort is drawn off and cooled before being transferred to a fermentation tank. Here, yeast is added. This is the beginning of fermentation, which will take place in two stages, one aerobically (open to the air) and the other anaerobic (without oxygen). In the first, the yeasts multiply. In the second, the yeasts feed on fermentable sugars (glucose, maltose, maltotriose) and produce alcohol and carbon dioxide. These yeasts also produce lots of aromatic compounds. The wort is converted into beer.

5. Maturation. The beer is kept for a minimum of one and up to several weeks in holding tanks at a temperature of around 32°F (0°C). This stage refines the young beer, which is known as green beer.

6. Filtration. The beer is ready. It is filtered to remove residual yeasts and impurities.

7. Conditioning. The beer is transferred into different containers: barrels, cans, or bottles. Some beers are fermented again in their container. When this is the case, the brewer adds some sugar and yeast just before conditioning. The beer is then kept several weeks at 77°F (25°C) to enable fermentation. This is why you may sometimes find a deposit of yeast at the bottom of some beers.

The color is determined during malting: pale, amber, or dark

The color of the beer depends on the intensity of the kilning of the barley grains at the end of germination. If it is gentle, the malt will give the beer a pale color (pale lager). If it is very advanced, it can go from caramelization to roasting and the malt will give the beer a darker color (amber, dark, or even black). Wheat beer, also known as white beer, is a different story: here, wheat is added during its preparation. Wheat, which is very rich in protein, gives the cloudy white color that is typical of wheat beer. People often think that dark beers contain more alcohol than wheat or pale ones. In fact, color has nothing to do with it. The alcohol content depends on the amount of sugar in the wort before fermentation. So, a wheat beer can be stronger than a brown ale or stout.

Each to their own grain

Worldwide, the main source of starch, and therefore of sugar, is malting barley. In Europe, it is the main cereal component of beer and is often complemented by wheat. In other regions of the world, it is complemented to a greater or lesser extent by other sources of starch: corn in America, rice in Asia, and sorghum in Africa, for example. This difference in the composition of malt contributes to the great diversity of beers throughout the world. Hops, yeast, and the wide variety of brewing techniques also have a role to play.

Trappist beers versus abbey beers

From the Middle Ages onward, beer production was developed largely in abbeys and monasteries by the Cistercian monks who lived and worked there. Through the sale of beer, they provided for the needs of the community and contributed to charities. Today, Trappist beers are still produced within abbey walls under the supervision of a monk; by contrast, abbey beers can be produced by breweries not owned by monks.

WHY DOES THE HEAD ON BEER LAST LONGER THAN THE FROTH ON SPARKLING WINE?

We can all agree that the head on beer is smoother and lasts longer than the froth on sparkling wine. Why is this? Because beer is made up of a richer matrix than sparkling wine, which is more refined. In fact, beer is made with several raw ingredients that are rich in proteins, organic acids, and minerals. This is why its head is more stable.

Barley wines: when beer takes on the characteristics of wine

Barley wines are drinks in which the yeasts and enzymes have broken down all the sugars present in the must. The result is beers that have an alcohol content of around 18 percent and the flavor of very dry wine.

The role of yeasts

As in any fermentation, yeast plays a vital role. Two types of yeasts can be identified, corresponding to the two main families of beers: lagers and ales.

For lagers, *Saccharomyces pastorianus* is favored. This yeast ferments at low temperature and has a tendency to sediment (the yeasts group together) at the end of fermentation. It also produces relatively few esters and makes light and thirst-quenching beers, such as pilsners.

For ales, *Saccharomyces cerevisiae* is favored. It produces beers that are more complex and aromatic and that often have a higher alcohol content.

For making non-alcoholic beers, an alternative to the use of costly technologies to remove the alcohol is to create fermentation using specific microorganisms that consume only a limited quantity of sugar, such as *Saccharomyces cerevisiae var. chevalieri*.

CIDER

For a long time, cider played a supporting role, but over the last few years, it has experienced an exciting revival. With the resurgence in popularity of traditional apple varieties, more complex aromas, and ageing, fermented apple juice is now full of surprises.

How is cider made?

1. Harvesting, washing, and "scratting" the apples. After the apples are harvested, they are carefully selected. They are then washed and "scratted"—ground down. They will spend an hour in a macerator to reveal their aromas.

2. Pressing. The apples are crushed in a press to squeeze out all their juice, which will macerate about five days in a clarification tank so that all the impurities fall to the bottom of the tank.

3. Alcoholic fermentation. First, the juice is separated from the impurities that have risen to the surface and fallen to the bottom of the tank. This clarified juice will ferment. The yeasts present will absorb the sugar and produce ethanol and carbon dioxide. Once the cider has attained the desired level of sugar, fermentation is stopped. It passes through a juice extractor, which removes all the yeasts and stops fermentation.
Fermentation can be activated with, among other things, the help of yeast-derived products rich in nutrients for fermenting yeasts, especially when the medium is deficient in nutrients.

4. Blending. As with cognac and wine, the cellar master will blend ciders from different vats to create the best possible recipe.

5. Bottling. The cider is bottled. Tasting can begin!

And what about the apple pomace? Is it thrown out?

No. As it actually contains a lot of nutrients, apple pomace is generally used to feed sheep, pigs, or cattle.

French cider versus English or American cider

- Apple varieties: in France, cider apples are both sweet and bitter. They are very tart and not very pleasant to eat raw. In England and the United States, they are sweeter and less tart.
- The quantity of apples used also varies. In France, cider comes only from apple must. By contrast, in England and the United States, cider may contain only 30 percent of must.
- In France, fermentation is slow and therefore at low temperature, while in England and the United States, it is faster and at a higher temperature.
- In France, sugar is left in the cider, in contrast to English and American cider, where fermentation is left to continue until it naturally ceases, even if this (often) means adding sugar later.

As a result, French cider is traditionally less alcoholic than English and American cider, but not necessarily any sweeter. The apple taste is also stronger in French cider. However, despite their different production techniques, the two types of cider increasingly resemble each other.

Vintage cider

Cider was never given the chance to age. Because of this, cider producers launched ciders for aging. Less sweet, with fine bubbles, these ciders develop surprising flavors. Give them a try.

Cider yeasts

As with wine and beer, yeasts can be added during the cider fermentation process. Of course, they serve to facilitate and stabilize fermentation. Some can also destroy the sulfur compound, that slightly rotten-egg smell that is apparent when apples are fermented. Other yeasts accentuate the fresh- or stewed-fruit aspect, the banana aroma, or floral aromas. In short, yeasts also add complexity.

Sweet, medium-dry, or dry: what characterizes cider?

Its sugar level and therefore its alcohol level. In fact, the drier a cider is, the more alcohol it contains. Here, again, fermentation is responsible. In contrast to dry cider, a sweet cider will not ferment as long, and the yeast will thus have less time to absorb the sugar and produce alcohol. Sweet cider has an alcohol content of less than 3 percent, while dry cider is around 5.5 percent.

What should you look out for when buying cider?

- 100 percent pure juice: this is important because sometimes cider can be made with must mixed with water. And, of course, the more the must is diluted, the less flavor it will have.
- Naturally sparkling: this means that no carbon dioxide has been added to the cider to make it fizzier.
- Unpasteurized: this ensures that you can enjoy the beneficial flora and other nutrients produced by the fermentation process.

WINE

It may accompany an elaborate meal or pre-dinner snacks around a coffee table. And in summer, it will be drunk as white or rosé, to which ice cubes may even be added. Matched with certain foods, it will reveal their flavors. And on special occasions, it sparkles! Red, white, or rosé, wine is part of our culture. Let's explore this fermented drink and its many secrets.

How is wine made?

1. The grapes are prepared. They are harvested when ripe: they should be neither too sour, nor too sweet. Then, they are sorted: rotten and overripe grapes, along with any leaves, are removed and discarded. Next comes destemming: the berries are separated from the rachis (the stem holding the grapes). Finally, the grapes are crushed to extract their juice.

2. Alcoholic fermentation. The bloom—the characteristic whitish film—found on the skin of grapes is where the indigenous yeasts are found that will ferment the grape must. At this stage, many wine estates also add other yeasts to stabilize fermentation. As they absorb the sugar in the grapes, these yeasts will produce ethanol and carbon dioxide. They are very sensitive and like moderate temperatures. Above 90°F (32°C), they will die; below 59°F (15°C), they will become inactive. The vat must therefore be kept at a regular temperature. Fermentation can be activated with, among other things, the help of yeast-derived products rich in nutrients for fermenting yeasts, especially when the medium is deficient in nutrients.

3. Malolactic fermentation. Here, it is not yeasts but good bacteria that are at work, converting malic acid into lactic acid. They give body to the wine and reduce its acidity, which is similar to that of green apple. This second fermentation is particularly important for red wines and is less so, or omitted, for white, rosé, and sparkling wines, where acidity is more desirable.

4. Maturation. The wine will age in barrels. At this stage, it is closely monitored and tasted at regular intervals by the cellar master. This is also when the wine is clarified, removing any remaining impurities that could make it cloudy. How? By adding protein to it so that the particles in suspension clump together. These proteins are introduced in the form of egg white or gelatin. Certain yeasts or their components (known as yeast derivatives) can also be used to help clarify the wine.

5. Bottling. Once bottled, the wine can be aged for years, if correctly stored. Beware, however, of the "taste of light," which wine can develop when exposed to light. Wine must be kept in the right conditions once it has been bottled: at a temperature of between 54 and 61°F (12 to 16°C), a humidity level of around 50 percent, lying down, and protected from light.

WHAT DOES IT MEAN WHEN A WINE IS MARKED AS 12.5 PERCENT?

This figure indicates the wine's alcohol content: 12.5 percent alcohol by volume (ABV). And what about the rest? Well, it's water.

What differentiates red, white, and rosé?

To produce red wine, the grape skins and pulp are mixed together for about ten days at the fermentation stage. For rosé, the skins and pulp are left to macerate no longer than twelve hours. The skin and pulp are then separated so that the juice begins to ferment. For white wine, there is no maceration. The white grapes or black grapes with white flesh are pressed to separate the juice from the skins. It is this clear juice alone that ferments to produce white wine.

AND WHAT ABOUT SPARKLING WINE?

In the traditional method, sparkling wine is made in the same way as other wine, except that a second fermentation occurs after the wine has been bottled. For this to happen, sugars and yeasts are added. This *tirage*, or second fermentation, creates the bubbles in the wine. During this process, the bottles are regularly shaken then turned upside down, enabling the lees to accumulate in the neck of the bottle. Next, this part is frozen, which creates a kind of ice plug that traps the deposits, then the neck of the bottle is "disgorged" of all its impurities. After all these stages, the corks can finally be placed in the bottles of sparkling wine!

The superpowers of wine yeasts

Saccharomyces cerevisiae is the main yeast responsible for alcoholic fermentation. Do you remember the name? Yes, it is the same yeast that is found in the fermentation of bread as well as of beer and liquors. In France, three hundred different strains of yeast have been identified that can be involved in winemaking, but there are many more.

What is less widely known is that other yeasts produce aromatic compounds that can influence the flavor of the wine. As they feed, these yeasts make alcohol, but they will also produce fermentation aromas: floral aromas, such as rose, and fruit ones, such as banana or peach, for example. There is also a second type of aroma, known as varietal, that is associated with a particular grape variety. In fact, these aromas are already present in the grape, but you cannot smell them; they are revealed by certain yeasts during fermentation—the flavors of grapefruit and passion fruit in Sauvignon blanc, for example. Some experts estimate that yeasts—these microorganisms just a few microns in size—are responsible for eighty percent of the aromatic compounds that we can smell in wine.

And even when they are inactive (or dead), these yeasts have properties. Added after fermentation, they release antioxidants that both enable the wine to be kept longer and soften the tannins, which may be too pronounced.

How are the yeasts selected?
Before they can select yeasts, the yeast producers first have to locate them. To do so, they visit vineyards and wine cellars, in search of these rare gems. They then compare several different ones to see which will be the most resistant and also the most able to carry out their task. They will then propagate the yeast in a suitable environment: in a small tank at the beginning, a huge one at the end. Inside a packet of yeast, there are several hundred million individual organisms, all identical.

American vines all over France
Phylloxera is to blame. In the late nineteenth century, this aphid arrived from the United States in the pocket of a winemaker and attacked French vines. Having tried everything to save their vineyards, but without success, the vine growers were forced to destroy all their vines. They replaced them with American plants, which were immune to the aphid, onto which they grafted their own varieties.

WINE IN FIGURES

2 ¼ lb. (1 kg): the quantity of grapes needed to make the equivalent of one bottle of wine, i.e. 75 cl. 60 gallons (227 liters): the capacity of a wine barrel. Italy is the biggest wine producer in the world, with a production of over 1.29 billion gallons (49.1 million hectoliters) in 2020. France is the second largest, producing over 1.22 billion gallons (46.4 million hectoliters) in 2020.

LIQUORS (DISTILLED SPIRITS)

The production of liquors dates back to the Middle Ages. In fact, it was in the tenth century that Arab alchemists developed the alembic (still) and produced their first liquors—highly alcoholic drinks that were believed to have therapeutic properties. However, it was not until the fifteenth century that the production of liquors was developed by monks, and it was they, during this period, who harnessed the power of plants and fruits.

Today, 6.6 billion gallons (250 million hectoliters) of liquors are produced around the world each year. They exist everywhere, from Chinese *baijiu*, Mexican tequila, Brazilian cachaça, and American bourbon to Russian vodka, French *gentiane*, Italian grappa, and Scotch whisky. Let's explore the world of liquors.

So, what exactly are liquors?

Unlike wine, beer, and cider, liquors are distilled after fermentation; that is, the alcohol produced by fermentation is extracted by a process of gradually heating and cooling the vapors in a still or a distillation column.

The alcohol vapor produced during heating also contains aromatic compounds from the raw ingredients and/or fermentation. This is what qualifies this distillate as a "liquor."

These very different alcohols are made from seeds, potatoes, or other vegetables, plants, and, of course, fruits.

THE SPIRIT OF DISTILLED SPIRITS

The term "spirits" comes from the Latin *spiritus*, which refers to the product of distillation perceived as the heart of the drink. Which, by extension, gives us *eau de vie* (water of life). In fact, many virtues are still attributed to liquor today. People often say that liquors help with digestion, for example. That is false. Alcohol actually slows down digestion by increasing the number of calories to be ingested. The fallacious belief is doubtless founded on the warm sensation that liquors produce when consumed.

The most commonly consumed liquors in the world

Whisky
This liquor is made from cereal grains such as malted barley, rye, and/or corn that is fermented using carefully selected yeasts before being distilled. It is mainly produced in Scotland, the United States, Canada, Ireland, and Japan. Although whisky (or whiskey—the spelling used for that made in the United States and Ireland) is the generic name given to the drink, it is also known as bourbon in the United States and Scotch when referring to whisky made in Scotland.

Rum
Rum is made from sugar cane that is crushed, fermented, then distilled. It is produced mainly in the Caribbean and Central America, but also throughout the world. It acquires an amber or brown color during the ageing phase in wooden barrels. Some runs are "white," indicating that they have not gone through this stage—or not for long.

Vodka
This alcohol results from the distillation of a fermented wort produced mainly from cereals such as wheat, barley, rye, and corn, but also, more rarely, various vegetables, such as potato, turnip, carrot, and, indeed, anything that can be fermented. The most famous vodkas are produced in Russia, Poland, and Finland. Vodka is distilled between three and six times. For this reason, when it leaves the stills, it can be up to 96 percent alcohol. In such cases, it needs to be mixed with water to be drinkable.

Gin
Gin is a drink resulting from the fermentation of malt (barley, rye, corn) or, as with vodka, anything else that can be fermented. Then, unlike vodka, numerous spices are added to the drink: juniper berries, coriander, fennel, licorice—anything is possible.

Tequila
Like mezcal, tequila is made from a plant called the blue agave, and in particular from its core. It is first heated and crushed before being fermented. As with rum, the paler tequila is, the less it has been aged. Some tequila is aged in old whisky barrels, which makes it more aromatic and means it should be drunk slowly.

THE ORIGINS OF THE TEQUILA SHOT

In 1930, to stem an epidemic of the Spanish flu in northern Mexico, doctors advised drinking tequila accompanied with lime and salt. And the tradition continued. However, if you are served a good tequila, savor it. Leave out the lime and salt, which will ruin all the aromas.

Baijiu

Baijiu is a Chinese liquor made from distilled cereals such as sorghum, rice, wheat, or barley. Unlike the previously mentioned liquors, *baijiu* is produced by mixed fermentation, incorporating a highly diverse microbial population. This alcohol is very popular in China. More than 2.6 billion gallons (10 billion liters) of *baijiu* are consumed every year. It is drunk down in one go and is very alcoholic.

Cognac (or brandy)

Here, it is grape must that is fermented for five to seven days. At this stage, the alcohol content of the wine is still low; it is the distillation and ageing in oak casks that will give this liquor all its aromatic strength and alcohol level.

Other fruit- and plant-based liquors

Pear, raspberry, plum, grape, apple, damson, cherry, banana, genepi, and gentian, not to mention the many blends: the world is full of fruit- and plant-based alcoholic beverages. As an example, it takes about 30 pounds (14 kg) of Bartlett (also known as Williams) pears to make 1 liter of Poire Williams liqueur.[51]

The main stages in making liquors

1. Preparation of the raw ingredients. When making a grain-based liquor, the first stage is malting. This is the case with whisky, which is started in the same way as beer—with malted barley. This malt is then ground, and the resulting "grist" is then mashed to produce the wort that will be fermented, as with beer. With fruit, vegetables, or herbs, there is obviously no need for malting.

2. Fermentation. It is during this stage that the sugars in the raw ingredients are converted into alcohol. Fermentation can last between a few hours and several days. At the end of the period, the resulting fermented liquid is known as "wash."

3. Distillation. This is the separation of water and alcohol, which happens in a still. As the wort is heated in the still, the alcohol molecules and aromatic compounds lighter than water molecules evaporate, because alcohol boils at around 158°F (70°C) rather than at 212°F (100°C) like water. The alcohol vapor then passes through a condenser surrounded by cold water and condenses and this distillate is then collected.

4. Maturation. This distilled spirit is placed in casks, vats (for large quantities), or demijohns (for small volumes). The aim is the same: to age the liquor. This stage is not essential: some alcohols, such as vodka, for example, do not need to be aged.

5. Blending. This stage concerns only fruit-based liquors such as Cognac, for example. The cellar master monitors the development of the liquor in the casks and produces blends.

The "angels' share"

When liquor is kept in casks, a proportion of the alcohol evaporates: this is known as the "angels' share." In general, this is estimated to be about 2 percent per year in Europe and 6 percent in tropical climates. This evaporation also provides favorable conditions for the fungus *Torula compniacensis*, which feeds on these alcohol vapors. This is the reason why there are blackened walls in liquor-producing towns like Cognac, for example—they are infested with this fungus.

The challenge of selecting yeasts for liquors

Alcohol is toxic not only for us but also for yeasts. When there is too much of it, they die. In order to ensure that fermentation is successful, therefore, yeast producers have the difficult task of finding yeasts that can hold their alcohol.

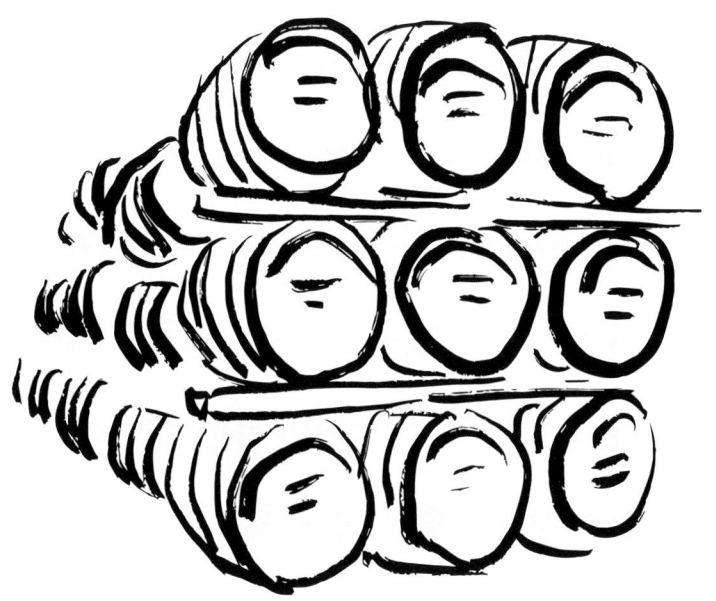

THE MANY VARIETIES OF FERMENTED FOODS

133

JENEVER
FRUIT WINE
VODKA
VODKA
BEER
VODKA
SLIVOVICA
RAKI
KVAS
TEA
BEER
KEFIR
TEA
BEER
SOJU
BEER
COFFEE
BEER
TEA
BAIJU
KOMBUCHA
SAKÉ
COFFEE
BEER
SORGHUM BEER
CIDER
BEER
RHUM
WINE
BEER
CIDER
WINE

KOMBUCHA

The story of kombucha
There are many legends surrounding kombucha. Although it is known to have existed in China in the second century BCE, it is believed to have come from Mongolia. In fact, traces of it have been found throughout Asia and in Russia.
Its origins, which remain shrouded in mystery, are claimed to involve Genghis Khan and the physician of a Chinese emperor. It is most likely that kombucha was not invented intentionally: tea forgotten in a jar would have produced microorganisms, which would have multiplied with the successive additions of other sweet teas.
Its name comes from the Japanese words *kombu*, meaning algae, and *cha*, tea. And although this really has nothing to do with our drink, it nevertheless remains the name by which it is commonly known.

What exactly is kombucha?
It is a sweetened black or green tea fermented by a SCOBY (symbiotic culture of bacteria and yeast) known as the "mother of kombucha." This viscous disk looks much like a mother of vinegar, the slimy deposit that forms in old vinegar that enables you to remake it. To make your own kombucha, you will first need to get hold of a mother.

You should also be aware that at some point during its fermentation, kombucha can contain alcohol. However, the alcohol, like the sugar, often breaks down as fermentation progresses.

What happens when you ferment kombucha?
Once the mother is placed into the tea, fermentation begins. Researchers have noted different types of symbiosis. The yeasts convert the sugar into alcohol and carbon dioxide, then the bacteria convert the sugar into acid. This is what gives kombucha its distinctive flavor.

YOU CAN EVEN MAKE CLOTHES FROM KOMBUCHA.

Suzanne Lee, a New York designer, specializes in them. In 2000, outraged by the highly polluting techniques used by the fashion industry, she started studying other means of creating clothing. And she hit on kombucha. In 2003, Lee launched Bio Couture, a brand of clothing made from strains of kombucha that she has grown. Today, she is continuing to research what could be the future of fashion.[52]

KOMBUCHA

Equipment
- A glass jar for the first fermentation
- A tight-knit piece of fabric held in place with an elastic band
- A bottle with a mechanical stopper for the second fermentation

Ingredients
- 1 tbsp black tea leaves
- 4 ¼ cups (2 pints/1 liter) boiling water
- Scant ½ cup (2 ¾ oz./80 g) sugar
- A kombucha mother or symbiotic cultures in liquid or dried form
- Scant ½ cup (3 ½ fl oz./100 ml) of the liquid surrounding the kombucha mother

WHAT ABOUT STORE-BOUGHT KOMBUCHA?

More and more brands, mostly organic, are offering kombucha. If you want to make the most of the drink's health benefits, choose unpasteurized kombucha. Pasteurization neutralizes the microorganisms that do you good and it can also affect the taste. By all means buy kombucha, but make sure it is alive.

First fermentation

1. Infuse the tea leaves in the boiling water and stir in the sugar. After 15 minutes, strain the tea into a glass jar.

2. Once the solution is cool, add the kombucha mother. The paler part of the mother should be facing upward, the darker part at the bottom of the jar.

3. Cover the jar with the piece of fabric, securing it with an elastic band, and let ferment for 1 week at room temperature and away from direct sunlight. The ideal temperature is around 72 to 74°F (22 to 23°C). Much higher and the SCOBY could deteriorate.

4. You can now drink your kombucha, unless you want it to be sparkling, in which case, continue with the second fermentation.

Where should the mother be?

In general, the mother floats to the surface. If it is in the middle of the liquid, that is not a problem; fermentation will continue. But if the kombucha sinks to the bottom and remains there several days, it is definitely dead. You will need to get hold of another one.

THE FOUR RULES FOR MAKING HOMEMADE KOMBUCHA

Avoid using metal utensils
Kombucha and metal utensils do not mix well. Metal can change the flavor of your kombucha and weaken the mother.

Start slowly
Kombucha is good for your health. It works on your microbiota to improve digestion. But because it contains lots of microorganisms, it is best to start with a small quantity, say a scant ½ cup (3 ½ fl oz./100 ml) per day. If you have no upset stomach, you can continue to drink it.

Don't forget your kombucha
If you let your kombucha ferment too long, it will develop a vinegary taste. Test it every other day, and when it is to your taste, place it in the fridge and fermentation will stop. You can then consume it within a month.

What if the kombucha mother becomes covered in mold and turns black?
If this happens, you will need to throw out both the drink and the mother because they have become oxidized.

Second fermentation

1. Pour the solution obtained from the first fermentation into a bottle, which will need to be sealed this time. This is the moment at which you can add another flavoring ingredient (see below). Seal the bottle but be sure to monitor it closely, as the gas produced can cause the bottle to explode. Every two days, release the gas and check to see if the kombucha is fizzy enough for your taste. When it is, you can place the bottle in the fridge to stop fermentation. Continue to release the gas daily.

2. Drink your kombucha within 1 month.

During this second fermentation, you can flavor your kombucha. Try ginger, blueberry, beet, lemon verbena, or even turnip. Anything is possible. Simply add some fruit, vegetable, or root juice or puree of your choice. In terms of quantity, it is a matter of taste, but a 1-inch (2.5-cm) piece of ginger, grated, or ten percent of fruit juice, or a handful of herbs, should suffice.

Once fermentation has ended

Your mother of kombucha is a living organism, so you need to feed it to keep it. Once you have prepared your drink, place the mother in a small bowl. Clean it with white vinegar then replace it into a solution of sugary tea. It should keep in this way for about 3 weeks.

MILK KEFIR

The story of milk kefir

Kefir is ancient: its earliest traces date back to 3500 BCE in the west of China and were discovered on a mummified body. This leads us to suppose that kefir was seen as an offering or as a provision to accompany the deceased into the afterlife. This would make milk kefir the earliest form of cheese in the world, much earlier than fermented rennet-based cheeses.

Milk kefir and water kefir

Although they may have the same name, milk kefir and water kefir have nothing to do with each other. The SCOBY—the mix of bacteria and yeast strains—of each is different and do not enable you to make the same drinks.

So, what is milk kefir?

It is a fermented drink made from kefir grains, which look like little cauliflowers. These grains are packed with bacteria and yeasts and are unlike any other SCOBY or symbiotic culture. Kefir can be used to make butter, cream, and fresh cheese (see the recipe opposite).

Kefir grains cannot be bought

Like those of water kefir, these kefir grains cannot be bought—that is the tradition. However, there are many Facebook groups that offer to put kefir grain donors and seekers in touch. No money changes hands; you simply send a self-addressed padded envelope along with an airtight freezer bag in which the donor can put the grains. When you receive them, place them in a jar filled with water and a spoonful of sugar. Then place the jar in the fridge, where the grains will happily wait a week before you are ready to make your kefir.

What happens when you make milk kefir?

As with kombucha or water kefir, fermentation begins as soon as the SCOBY is put in contact with a sweet liquid, in this case milk. The bacteria feed on the sugars and produce carbon dioxide, as with a sourdough starter. This gives the drink its sour and fizzy taste.

MILK KEFIR

Equipment
- A fine-mesh sieve
- A 1 ½-quart (1.5-liter) jar with a lid
- 1-quart (1-liter) bottle with a mechanical stopper

Ingredients
- 4 ¼ cups (2 pints/1 liter) milk (unpasteurized or pasteurized; UHT milk, which is sterilized, contains fewer nutrients)
- 1 tbsp kefir grains

WHAT DO YOU DO WITH THE KEFIR GRAINS AFTERWARD?

You can use them again immediately or store them in milk in the fridge. Remember to change the milk from time to time so that the grains can continue to feed.

1. If you are using unpasteurized milk, boil then cool it before use, or your kefir won't be smooth.

2. Pour the kefir grains into a jar, pour in the milk, then cover the jar, but don't seal it.

3. Leave at room temperature (between 64 and 75°F/18–24°C) for 24 to 48 hours, shaking the jar occasionally. The liquid will thicken and become more acidic.

4. Strain the liquid into a mixing bowl to retrieve the kefir grains. You can drink the kefir straight away or ferment it again to make it fizzy. Pour the grain-free drink into an airtight bottle this time and let it ferment in the fridge for 24 hours.

Variation: kefir fresh cheese

1. To make fresh cheese, ferment the milk kefir with the grains for 36 to 48 hours.

2. Strain out the grains.

3. Pour the kefir into a sieve lined with cheesecloth over a bowl.

4. Let drain at room temperature, checking for the desired consistency. As a guide, you will have a soft cheese after about 18 hours. The longer you leave it, the more mature it will be.

WATER KEFIR OR TIBICOS

The story of water kefir
The origins of water kefir grains remains a mystery. Strains are believed to have been found in South America and Tibet, but this has not been confirmed. Like milk kefir and kombucha, water kefir was probably not created intentionally. It is likely that the dregs of sugar water left in a gourd over the years produced a culture of bacteria and yeasts.

What is water kefir?
Water kefir is a fermented drink made from a culture of water kefir grains—microorganisms that are also known as SCOBY. As with kombucha, you cannot create this culture. To make water kefir, you first need to obtain some water kefir grains, then, to keep them, "feed" them with a sugar solution (see p. 144).

What happens when you make water kefir?
As with kombucha, once the water kefir grains are immersed in sugar water they feed on the sugar. After 48 hours, only 20 percent of the original quantity of sugar will remain.

THE ORIGIN OF THE WORD KEFIR

Kefir comes from the word *kefi*, meaning "of choice" or "quality" in the Caucasian region.

WATER KEFIR

Equipment
- A fine-mesh sieve
- A 1 ½-quart (1.5-liter) jar with a lid
- 1-quart (1-liter) bottle with a mechanical stopper

Ingredients
- 1 tbsp kefir grains
- 4 ¼ cups (2 pints/1 liter) water (if it is chlorinated, let rest a while so that the chlorine evaporates)
- ¼ cup (1 ¾ oz./50 g) cane sugar
- 1 dried fig
- A handful of raisins
- ¼ lemon
- Fruit for flavoring—try half a lemon, or other fruits, herbs, or roots, such as ginger, berries, melon, basil, etc.

AND WHAT DO YOU DO WITH THE KEFIR GRAINS AFTERWARD?

The kefir grains will keep for over a month if stored in the fridge in a light sugar solution. Remember to top up with water from time to time. Alternatively, you can dry them. Simply add a little sugar water to the dried grains and they will come back to life. You can then use them for another fermentation.

1. Place the kefir grains in a jar and pour in the water.

2. Add the sugar, fig, raisins, and lemon.

3. Place the lid over the jar but don't seal it.

4. Let ferment for 24 to 48 hours, until the fig floats to the surface.

5. Strain through a fine-mesh sieve over a bowl to retrieve the grains.

6. At this stage, you can add some fruit or vegetable puree or juice or some herbs to your kefir to flavor it. Allow a scant ¼ cup (50 ml) of puree or juice per 4 ¼ cups (2 pints/1 liter) of kefir.

7. Pour everything into a bottle, seal, and let stand at room temperature for a further 24 hours. The kefir will now be loaded with carbon dioxide.

8. Your kefir is now ready to drink. Store it in the fridge and drink it within 1 month. Don't forget to release the gas regularly to prevent the bottle exploding as a result of carbon dioxide buildup.

Tip
The dried fig accelerates fermentation of the water kefir and the raisins contain yeasts that facilitate fermentation of the kefir.

GINGER BUG OR GINGER STARTER

Like kombucha and kefir, ginger bug serves as a starter for many types of drinks. Because of its ginger flavor, it also enables you to make ginger beer. This well-known drink has a very fresh, sometimes almost apple-like, taste. Like all fermented drinks, it is not too sweet, which is another of its advantages.

What happens when you make ginger bug?
Rather than a SCOBY, this drink uses a starter—a culture of microorganisms that are introduced to a product to create fermentation. Starters are not only used for making bread. Here, the microorganisms are bacteria present on the skin of ginger (as on grape skins for making wine) that will feed on sugar, multiply, and produce gas.

GINGER BUG

Equipment
- A sealable jar

Ingredients
- 1 cup (½ pint/250 ml) water
- Several tbsp of white or brown sugar
- Several tbsp of finely chopped ginger

1. Put the water, a tablespoon of sugar, and a tablespoon of finely chopped ginger into a jar with a sealable lid.

2. Seal the jar and put it in a warm place, such as on a radiator or in direct sunlight. Here, unlike with symbiotic cultures, or SCOBY, there is no risk of the temperature getting too high. On the contrary.

3. After 24 hours, add another tablespoon of finely chopped ginger and of sugar to your drink. Shake the jar and put it back in the same place.

4. Repeat this process every 24 hours. The drink should become opaque and bubbles should appear. This will usually take 4 or 5 days, depending on the temperature.

5. Once your ginger bug is ready, you can add it to fruit juice to make a fizzy drink.

6. If you feed your ginger bug with ginger and sugar once a month, it will keep in the fridge virtually indefinitely. When you want to reactivate it, simply move it to a warm place and start feeding it every 24 hours, as described above.

GINGER BEER

Equipment
- A sealable jar
- A clean kitchen towel
- A bottle with an airtight cap

Ingredients
- 4 ¼ cups (2 pints/1 liter) boiling water
- 1 ¾ oz. (50 g) fresh ginger, peeled and finely chopped
- ¼ cup (1 ¾ oz./50 g) superfine sugar
- Scant ¼ cup (2 fl. oz./50 ml) lemon juice
- Scant ¼ cup (2 fl. oz./50 ml) ginger bug

1. Pour the water into a saucepan and add the ginger. Simmer for 15 minutes.

2. Add the sugar and lemon juice and pour into a jar.

3. Let cool before adding the ginger bug. Immediately replace the amount taken out with the same quantity of sugar water.

4. Shake the jar well, cover with a clean kitchen towel, and let ferment at room temperature until bubbles appear.

5. As soon as the "beer" is clearly foaming, strain it. You can now bottle it. If you want it to become more alcoholic, let it ferment at room temperature. When the bubbling slows down, pour it into a bottle.

6. You can enjoy your drink immediately or leave it in the fridge to ferment a second time. But don't forget to open the bottle regularly to release the carbon dioxide, or the bottle may explode.

FERMENTATION AND OUR SENSES

Immersing yourself in sensory analysis is about exploring your history, your senses, and your culture, both personal and collective. Tasting a dish while concentrating on everything that you are sensing is a thrilling experience that you can indulge in throughout the following pages, where you will discover the favorite food-and-drink pairings of some top chefs.

Happy tasting!

THE THEORY OF FOOD PAIRING

Text written from interviews with **Agnès Giboreau**, Director of Research at **Institut Paul Bocuse** and a specialist in food evaluation.

You don't need to be an expert to understand the basics of sensory analysis. Take a slice of fresh bread, for example: a food that is flavorsome, has a characteristic taste, and is easy to get hold of. Now let's examine the various stages of tasting in order to understand what lies behind this "taste."
First of all, there is the specific shape of the type of bread you are eating, which will immediately evoke memories of fresh bread, making this one either appetizing or unappealing. There is also the characteristic smell, which will continue to stimulate your senses. The sound of the knife cutting through the crust and then the crumb of the loaf will heighten your anticipation and boost (or not) your desire to consume it. Once you bite into it, you will become aware, almost simultaneously, both of the contrasting textures of the crust and the crumb and of the taste of the bread: slightly salty, with notes of wheat, yeast, and perhaps a hint of caramel. This "taste" is a combination of the flavors you perceive on your tongue (sourness, for example) and the aromas you perceive with your nose (toasty, for example).
Sight, hearing, touch, smell, taste: all our senses come into play when we taste a dish. But that's not all: studies have shown that the appreciation of a meal is also a cultural and personal matter. Criteria such as an individual's history, biological makeup, and origins also play an important part. Let's explore sensory analysis.

THE SENSES INVOLVED BEFORE AND WHILE YOU EAT

BEFORE YOU EAT

The moment before you take a bite of food is an essential one. Eating is an intimate act, because you are incorporating a foreign body into your own. For this reason, it is important that you really want to do so. This is the "role" of the moment immediately before you take a bite.

Sight. Everything begins with this sense. Thanks to sight, your brain will envisage tasting and prepare to activate your tastebuds. Sight enables you to anticipate a pleasurable experience, thereby influencing your expectations. But beware: if the taste does not match what you see on your plate, the experience could be spoilt. For example, if you are presented with an orange-colored soup, you will immediately remember the taste of carrot or pumpkin. But if it turns out to be cauliflower, you will be so surprised that you may no longer be able to appreciate the soup—especially if you are particularly partial to carrot or pumpkin soup! Sight enables you to preconstruct the anticipated sensory experience, in terms of its taste but also its smell, texture, and even temperature.

Smell. This sense is first involved when the dish is presented to you, before you actually taste it. Like sight, smell is a powerful stimulus to make you want to eat (or not). Its role becomes even more important later, once you have the food in your mouth.

Touch. Here, this sense interacts with hearing. It is when you touch a food that you perceive its texture. This may cause a sound (like the crunch of the crust of bread when you cut it). Again, if it is not in line with what you imagined, you may be disappointed with the food, but, of course, touch can also stimulate your desire to consume it.

WHILE YOU EAT

Touch. In the mouth, touch involves chewing. So, if the bread is soft on your teeth, you may be disappointed, especially if this is not how you imagined it. On the other hand, the contrast between the crumb and the crust when you bite into it may confirm the expected crunch. As you are chewing, the food in your mouth is transformed by the action of your teeth and saliva. The tactile receptors in the mouth and palate will then inform you of the texture of the bread: airy, springy, or soft.

Taste and smell. For the uninitiated, it is very difficult to differentiate between these two senses, which come into play when you savor food. When you put food into your mouth, it is your tastebuds that detect the flavors of sourness, bitterness, sweetness, and saltiness. Specialists have added to this list umami, which can be found in stock or fish sauces, and more recently, oleogustus: the taste of fat. Everything else is down to smell. So, it is thanks to the air that naturally circulates between the nose and the mouth that we know that this sweet-and-sour fruit is a strawberry, for example. Without sight and smell, it is impossible to know what you are eating, like when you have a cold. In the mouth, a third sensory circuit comes into play: the trigeminal nerve. It is this nerve that detects the spiciness of pepper and the fizziness of a soda.

IF YOU HAVE EATEN SOMETHING TOO SPICY, EATING RICE WILL DO NOTHING TO HELP YOU.

It is often said that to counteract the effects of eating a spicy dish, you should eat rice or drink a glass of milk. But this is a myth. In fact, the trigeminal nerve is sensitive only to the sensation of spiciness; eating another food that it is insensitive to will therefore not solve the problem. You simply need to stop eating the spicy food and the sensation will pass.

CRITERIA BEYOND YOUR CONTROL

You will doubtless have noticed that when you taste a dish, how you imagine it and the sensation in your mouth are not the only determining factors in the experience. Your whole being is involved.

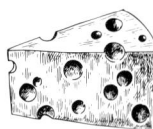

Culture. This is a very important factor in the taste experience. For example, the French eat a lot of cheese—fermented dairy products—which might be repellent in Asia, where cheese is rare. Conversely, Asian fermented fish, which adds a lot of flavor to stocks, may disgust the French. During the tasting experience, it is important to bear this cultural dimension and your openness to new food experiences in mind. It is possible to learn to appreciate an unknown food. Eaten often enough, it will become familiar, and you might even grow to like it.

Personal history. "I don't like spinach." "I love all green vegetables." Of course, taste is a matter of personal preference, but we, and our tastes, are also the products of our environment. A baby's tastes begin to develop while they are still in their mother's womb. So, if your mother had a passion for spinach while she was pregnant with you, there is a likely chance that you will share her tastes, especially as spinach is often one of the first solid foods babies are introduced to. We are not all equal faced with a plate of spinach. Fortunately, the way it is cooked can help all of us to appreciate it.

The moment. You have doubtless had the experience of being on vacation and trying a local wine. It is the end of the day, the weather is balmy, you are in good company, and you are feeling relaxed. The wine is delicious, incredible even. Happy with your discovery, you take a bottle home with you to enjoy with friends. But back home, what an anticlimax: the wine is actually very mediocre. The moment changed your perception of the product. This is the reason why fine dining restaurants pay meticulous detail to the ambience of the setting: the pleasurable experience begins as soon as you walk into the restaurant. When you are analyzing a dish, it is therefore important to extricate yourself from elements that could intrude on your tasting experience.

THE DIFFERENT WAYS OF PAIRING FOOD

Based on the thesis by **Anastasia Eschevins**, *"Les accords bières et mets, de la perception au jugement des consommateurs en situation réelle de repas" (Beer and food pairings, from perception to consumer assessment in a real meal situation), supervised by* **Catherine Dacremont**, *CSGA, Université de Dijon, and* **Agnès Giboreau**, *IPBR, Université Lyon 1 - Fonds Baillet Latour.*

Bear in mind that food pairings are based on three basic principles: similarity, complementarity, and contrast. However, these principles are not set in stone and research is constantly evolving in accordance with changing eating and drinking habits.

Similarity. Whether the similarity is olfactory, visual, or linked to origin, pairing products that share the same identity always works. For example, two citrus fruits, two products sharing the same cellar fermentation, or a wine with spicy notes accompanying a spicy dish will always be a successful pairing.

Complementarity. Some flavors complement each other. Whether it is the fatty taste of a product offset by something dry, or sourness balanced with sweetness, two very different elements can combine to provide a unified taste experience, in other words, one that integrates all the taste sensations so that you can no longer really determine which element provides which taste.

Contrast. Both within a dish and when creating a menu, it is also important to create contrasts. Experts have highlighted the phenomenon of specific sensory satiation: if you always eat the same thing or if your plate contains only one type of food, you are likely to have had your fill more quickly than if your plate includes various elements. It can therefore be interesting to pair a drink and a dish that provide sensory variety.

WHAT DO YOU DO IF YOU ARE NOT AN EXPERT?

Sensory analysis is not just for experts. Or so Agnès Giboreau, Director of Research at the Institut Paul Bocuse, maintains. While you are tasting a food or dish, the important thing is to concentrate on your sensations and to try to be as objective as possible. Here are a few of her tips for doing so.

Tip n° 1. Regularly organize blind tastings using opaque containers. The fact that you cannot see the food you are eating will prevent you being influenced in the descriptions you give of it. Experiments have shown that testers chose adjectives relating to pale foods to describe white tea when they could see what they were tasting but not when the tasting was blind.

Tip n° 2. Blind tasting is easier when there are two of you. One can prepare the food, while the other tastes it. You can choose a ready-prepared drink or food (for example a plain or fruit yogurt) or experiment in the kitchen by adding spices, sauces, and other ingredients. If you are blind tasting on your own, you could prepare several dishes ahead of time, placing codes combining numbers and letters on them that will be difficult for you to memorize.

Tip n° 3. Start with very different samples. As you progress in tasting, choose products with similar tastes to sharpen your senses.

Tip n° 4. Note what immediately comes to mind without looking to rationalize your responses. Your descriptions might be very pictorial: a wine that tastes like volcanic soil, for example. The "right" answer will be the one you manage to find. Feel free to use lots of descriptive terms. As you progress with the tastings, you will begin to become more specific.

Tip n° 5. Share your impressions. You will need to combine several elements to build an identity that can be shared: one person's words can be adopted by the other. Later, you can also draw inspiration from guides on tasting vocabulary, which will enable you to rely on commonly accepted terms.

FERMENTED FOOD AND DRINK PAIRINGS

By the **Institut Paul Bocuse**'s experts.

PAIRING PORT WITH ROQUEFORT

By **Gaëtan Bouvier**, Master of Port 2019, Best Sommelier of France 2016.

I love creating a surprise with this pairing. It's an almost algorithmic love match, combining foods that humans have consumed since time immemorial (bread, wine, cheese, and fruit) in a way that is simple yet sophisticated. When I have guests, I like to offer them this simple pairing rather than a plethora of cheeses on a board.

PORT

What you need to know about port—the result of centuries of expertise—is that it is one of the greatest wines in the world. It combines the jovial appeal of sugar with the heady power of mutage and the wisdom of time, with its long cellar aging.

The fermentation of port

Fermentation of port begins like that of wine, but when the wine reaches 6 percent alcohol, 77 percent grape liquor is added to it, which has the effect of stopping the initial fermentation. This process is known as mutage. This is why port usually contains about 20 percent alcohol and is quite sweet. It is then bottled and aged in cellars.

For this pairing, I chose a twenty-year-old Tawny port, which has a Chinese-red color with amber reflections, numerous languid and slow legs, a shiny meniscus, and a slightly transparent appearance. The nose is powerful and warm, full of complex aromas of walnut, honey pastries, toasted almond, date, prunes in brandy, milk chocolate, turmeric, and saffron. The smooth, creamy mouthfeel combines the sweet flavor of residual sugar, the warmth of the mutage alcohol, the tartness of the volatile acids from long aging, and complex tertiary aromas following the oxidation from casking.

ROQUEFORT

Creamy white in color, with blue veining generated by the yeast known as *Penicillium roqueforti*, crumbly and firm. The nose has a pronounced ovine smell, a spicy trigeminal sensation, and a powerful and very intense aromatic bouquet of cellar, rye, farm, and rancid milk. The mouthfeel—creamy, salty, spicy, and strong, with pronounced aromas—leaves a long-lasting aromatic finish.

Why does it work?
Although they don't come from the same country, these two products have certain things in common. Both are agricultural products having undergone different fermentations, so they obviously have a lot to say to each other. All six taste modalities can be found here: sourness, bitterness, sweetness, saltiness, umami, and—the final one—oleogustus.

The appealing sweetness of the port is balanced by the saltiness of the Roquefort. The bitterness of the alcohol contributed by the fortifying grape liquor complements the sourness of the cheese. The fermentation provides umami, that indefinable but very interesting flavor. Oleogustus, from the milk fat in the Roquefort, like the icing on the cake, adds the final touch to this pairing.

In my line of work, we measure length—the persistence of the aromas. Roquefort has a length of eighteen, while port has twenty. These two products therefore work very well together, even in terms of their long finish.

How to drink port
- I recommend drinking it in a wine glass with a wide bowl, at 57°F (14°C), as for most wines.
- Top-quality port wines are worth taking time to observe, smell, and savor attentively.
- I recommend a serving quantity of 2 ¾ fl. oz. (80 ml), which allows you to stay within the limits in terms of alcohol absorption and calories. My motto: "Less but better."

TOASTED RYE BREAD WITH ROQUEFORT
AND CHERRIES GLAZED WITH SHERRY VINEGAR

Serves 4

For the toasted rye bread
- 1 tsp churned butter
- A round loaf of rye bread cut into ¾-inch (2-cm) slices

For the Roquefort topping
- 5 oz. (150 g) Roquefort
- 1 ½ tbsp crème fraîche

For the cherries in sherry vinegar
- 7 oz. (200 g) Burlat cherries
- Scant ½ cup (3 ½ fl. oz./100 ml) sherry vinegar
- A pinch of salt

GAËTAN BOUVIER'S RECOMMENDED PAIRING:

Ramos Pinto twenty-year-old Tawny Porto.

Gaëtan BOUVIER's recipe

1. In a skillet, heat the butter until it turns a nut-brown color. Toast the slices of bread in the pan on both sides.

2. Mix the Roquefort and cream until you have a smooth paste.

3. In a saucepan, heat the sherry vinegar until just simmering.

4. Pit the Burlat cherries, then pour the simmering vinegar over them and leave to macerate for 18 hours.

To serve

1. Spread the Roquefort mixture on the toasted rye bread.

2. Arrange the vinegar-marinated cherries on top.

3. Coat the cherries with the remaining marinade.

SHU PU'ER CHA WITH TOMME DE SAVOIE IGP AU FOIN

By **Bernard Ricolleau**, Institut Paul Bocuse hotel manager and tea specialist.

In France, when we speak of tea, we naturally think of Ceylon black teas or of green teas you drink from large cups. As I got interested in this product, I discovered that there are many teas that lend themselves perfectly to drinking with savory dishes. As an alternative to wine—which I also appreciate—I find tea fascinating. The variety that I've chosen is pu'er. I like its full-bodied, atypical taste. It truly is a tea to drink with a meal and has an unsettling taste, which of course makes it very interesting.

SHU PU'ER CHA*

Pu'er tea is a dark fermented tea that is little-known outside of China, which has long kept its treasures to itself. It comes from Yunnan province, to the west of Hong Kong, where it is consumed all day long. However, it is alien to our European drinking habits. And with good reason, because it is fermented. It has a musky, tertiary, almost animal flavor. Its woody notes evoke moss and undergrowth. Unlike other teas, which are kept in a very dry place, it is aged in a cellar, like wine. There are even vintage pu'ers. I've tasted a twenty-year-old pu'er that had aged like a very good wine and was exceptionally fine.

Be careful not to confuse the shu pu'er cha described here with shēng pu'er cha, which is a non-fermented green tea.

The fermentation of pu'er

Pu'er is a fermented tea. Its production starts with meticulous harvesting: only the buds and first leaves of the tea are picked. These leaves are then heated in a wok, as for green tea, then rolled ready to be dried. This stage is known as *sha qing*, or "killing the green."

The tea then begins to develop its character. After a few days—and this is the stage that differentiates pu'er from other black teas—it is placed in a pile that is then dampened and covered with a tarpaulin. In this humid, airless environment, which is conducive to the development of microbes, fermentation begins. This stage lasts between thirty and forty-five days. The pu'er is then molded, pressed with a millstone, and steamed to produce the different forms it is sold in. It is ready for its long journey of storage and aging, where its aromas will improve over time.

TOMME DE SAVOIE IGP AU FOIN

For this pairing with the pu'er tea, I chose Tomme de Savoie IGP au Foin. Made with unpasteurized whole cow's milk, it has a strong taste of freshly cut hay and walnuts. The rind is ivory yellow, quite thick, and particularly tasty. The cheese originated when farmers would store their wheels of cheese in hay to save space, which enabled the cheese to age and helped the hay to dry out.

Here, the lactic fermentation of the hay matches that of the cheese. The hay permeates the rind of the tomme, diffusing its notes in the pu'er tea.

Why does it work?

The aim of this pairing is not to have two contrasting tastes, but rather two strong identities that enhance each other. Both these products have powerful flavors with woody and earthy notes. In the mouth, you discover the aromas of undergrowth and cut grass from the hay and the tea. They have in common the animal and musky character of fermentation, with nuances of vanilla and licorice. The fatty and rich texture of the tomme marries perfectly with the silky consistency and intense taste of the tea. Two words, common to both these products, describe this pairing well: fermentation and vegetal. They are made for each other: tea that has matured, but whose leaves have truly asserted themselves during fermentation, and hay that has matured in the barn. The transversality of this pairing reveals a history and a marriage of two very different traditions.

MY TIPS

1. The water in the teapot. This should be no hotter than 176°F (80°C). The hotter the water is, the more it will accentuate the tea's bitter notes.

Preparing the tea following the *gongfu cha* method

Traditionally Chinese, *gong fu cha* is not strictly speaking a tea ceremony but rather a tasting method. To follow it, let the tea infuse twice, five seconds each time, then discard the water. You can drink the third infusion, which should be left to infuse longer—a minute to a minute and a half. This method allows the tea to open up like a good wine that could be decanted to allow it to express itself more fully.

Preparing an infusion at room temperature

You can also infuse pu'er at room temperature, which enables you to control the level of bitterness that develops in hot water. Simply infuse about a tablespoon of tea in 2 cups (17 fl. oz./500 ml) of room-temperature water for 45 minutes.

2. Wine glass. Better than a cup, a glass will not only enable you to appreciate the color of the tea, with its reflections, clarity, and brilliance, but will also enhance the tea's rich aromas.

How to best enjoy this pairing

To start with, I recommend that you prepare your palate by taking a small sip of tea and then eating a piece of the tomme. Then drink some more tea.

You can accompany this tasting with a light bread roll with subtle grain aromas and a slightly crispy crust.

CURDS WITH HAY

By **Florent Boivin**, Meilleur Ouvrier de France 2011, Head of Education at the Institut Paul Bocuse.

I love this pairing as it reminds me of a recipe that I spent a year developing for the Maison Troisgros near Roanne. Michel, the chef, wanted me to work with curd. So, I analyzed everything to do with this recipe until I got the texture I was looking for. I carried out scientific research on the type of rennet (an animal-based milk coagulant), the breed of dairy cow, the fermentation time, the ideal temperature—without success. Then, one day, as I was about to throw out some curd that I had forgotten about at the back of the fridge, the chef asked me if he could taste it. And he loved it! The consistency was perfect. I have very fond memories of that moment. This recipe is directly inspired by it.

CURD

I don't eat cheese but I am very drawn to milk because I spent my childhood making cheeses with my grandmother. I've always found it incredible how many products can be made with a single ingredient. This fermentation technique is universal and very accessible. The curd that I have made should be eaten at room temperature, which will bring out its clean but sweet tanginess. It has the texture of panna cotta and the taste of fromage blanc. The first impression in the mouth is gelatinous before softening. It is very supple: you can even make ravioli from it. (For more on how to make curd, see the recipe on page 166.)

How to make curd

Curdling is an acidification of milk that will destabilize its structure and gradually make it congeal. You can make curd in two different ways: by allowing the milk to acidify naturally or by adding an enzyme. The first method involves leaving it up to nature. The lactic enzymes naturally present in milk will feed on the lactose and transform it into lactic acid. Acidity will develop and the milk will curdle. The second method involves adding an enzyme in the form of rennet to the milk. Present in the stomach of unweaned calves, kids, and lambs, this enzyme has the ability to make milk coagulate. Florent Boivin opted for this method because it produces a firmer and therefore more manageable curd.

HAY

This is what gives the curd its flavor. I use hay from Crau (foin de Crau, AOC). It does not contain pesticides and is comprised of a balanced mix of grasses, legumes, and various plants. You can identify it by its characteristic red and white string. It adds a toasty flavor and gives the milk a complex aromatic profile.

Why does it work?

Milk is the main ingredient in this recipe; everything else is there to enhance it. The curd adds fat and a little sourness; the hay adds a fresh, herbal touch. These two products have the same roots. When you taste this curd infused with hay, the pairing seems obvious. To give it texture, I decided to accompany it with ravioli made from the top layer of the curd. I also add some béchamel sauce, which, again, recalls the lactic nature of this recipe. Finally, for freshness, asparagus completes this spring dish and adds some texture. A monochrome dish in which milk is the star. As a variation, you could also add some truffle for a perfect pairing.

HAY-INFUSED CURD WITH ASPARAGUS

Serves 8

For the curd
- 4 ¼ cups (2 pints/1 liter) fresh whole milk
- A handful of Crau hay (from a garden center or pet store) or a high quality hay suitable for cooking
- Some rennet (for quantity, check the indications on the bottle)

For the béchamel sauce with Parmesan
- ¼ cup (2 ¼ oz./60 g) butter
- Scant ⅔ cup (2 oz./60 g) all-purpose flour
- 3 cups + 3 tbsp (1 ½ pints/750 ml) fresh whole milk
- Generous ¾ cup (3 oz./80 g) grated Parmesan cheese

To finish
- 4 white asparagus spears
- 1 lemon
- Olive oil
- Parmesan shavings

HOTEL MANAGER BERNARD RICOLLEAU'S RECOMMENDED PAIRING:

Bancha Hojicha, a toasted green tea from Japan. The Hojicha tea adds herbal notes with toasted and tertiary flavors, while also contributing the freshness you would expect from a green tea that accompanies asparagus perfectly.

Florent BOIVIN's recipe

1. Pour the milk onto the (washed) hay and let infuse overnight. Strain the milk to remove the hay. Heat the milk to 99°F (37°C).

2. Turn off the heat, then stir in the rennet (following the indications on the bottle).

3. Place a stainless-steel frame lined with plastic wrap on a baking sheet. Pour the milk mixture into the frame to a height of ½ inch (1 cm). Let curdle at room temperature about 20 minutes.

4. Remove the frame and lay a damp, clean kitchen towel on top of the curd. Turn it out onto a wire rack and let drain overnight. The next day, cut it into rectangles, then refrigerate.

5. To make the sauce, melt the butter in a saucepan then stir in the sieved flour.

6. Cook the roux over low heat for about 5 minutes. Gradually add the cold milk, stirring continually, and bring to a boil.

7. Let cook for 5 minutes, then turn off the heat and stir the Parmesan in. Check the seasoning.

8. Peel the asparagus spears and slice them finely lengthwise using a mandoline.

9. Season with the lemon juice and olive oil.

10. Place a rectangle of curd on a hot plate, cover with some béchamel, and fold it over on itself.

11. Finish with some asparagus and Parmesan shavings, a few drops of olive oil, and some lemon zest.

How to best enjoy this dish
As it is, eaten with a spoon, or on a slice of French sourdough with a dense and soft crumb. What is important here is the texture: the béchamel will be soft but quite warm and enveloping. The curd will be lukewarm and soft, but much firmer. And eating it with a spoon will enhance all these sensations. Working with texture does not necessarily mean adding crunchy and liquid elements.

MALABAR COFFEE WITH CAMEMBERT

By **Alain Dauvergne**, Head Barman and Mixologist Bar Manager at the Institut Paul Bocuse.

A characterful cheese, a good French sourdough, and a cup of hot coffee: these are memories that, even today, inspire my research into surprising food-and-drink pairings. Coffee is an inexhaustible source of complex aromas and flavors. And we don't need to limit ourselves to the main arabica and robusta species. Each comprises a multitude of varietals—bourbon, typica, and caturra are just a few examples—which, shaped by their different terroirs, are capable of expressing more than a thousand aromas. A vast arena to which the great variety of cheeses can only participate.

MALABAR COFFEE

In the eighteenth century, this Indian coffee used to travel to Europe by sailboat, a journey that would last six months. It was not long before people realized that, during the long voyage, a second fermentation would take place inside the burlap sacks in contact with the ocean spray. Today, it is this very distinctive second fermentation that is reproduced, giving Malabar coffee a rather tart taste but also its grassy, undergrowth, fresh flavors. Its full-bodied flavor is due to its terroir, which tends to produce a coffee packed with essential oil. Particular attention is paid to the picking of the coffee cherries, which is done by hand. Unlike mechanical picking, this enables only the ripe cherries, which better reveal their aromas, to be picked.

The fermentation of Malabar coffee

The first fermentation is typical of washed coffee: the coffee cherries and grains are left to soak in water to break down the pulp. This pulp is then fermented a second time: the coffee is stored in bags that are only partially filled. The aim is to allow the moisture-laden monsoon air to circulate between the grains. This process lasts about seven weeks, during which time the coffee acquires all its flavor.

CAMEMBERT

Naturally, I recommend you choose Normandy AOP Camembert made from unpasteurized milk, as this is the most complex and aromatic kind. It should be ripened to the core, with a pale yellow color and slightly salty taste, and its rind should be streaked with white. For this pairing, you can choose a Camembert to suit your taste, but ideally it should not be too ripe, or its taste risks overpowering that of the coffee. It should be creamy and slightly bitter.

Why does it work?

With its rich and grassy notes, Malabar coffee is difficult to appreciate if you drink it on its own. It develops subtly spiced aromas with pepper and cinnamon flavors. You may also discover delicate notes of leather and cut grass. In this pairing, the thick rind of the Camembert—a result of fermentation—complements the cut-grass and woody notes of the coffee. The fattiness of the coffee blends with that of the cheese. The spicy notes present in the coffee, such as cinnamon and pepper, link the two products and help create a unified taste. Here, you cannot distinguish which element adds which taste, and that is precisely what makes this pairing so successful.

MY TIPS

1. The quantity of coffee. In my opinion, the ideal quantity of coffee is 2 ¼ oz. (60 g) for 4 ¼ cups (2 pints/1 liter) of water. If you add more, the coffee notes will be too pronounced. Less, and it will be under extracted.

2. The type of coffee maker. I would not recommend using an espresso machine because the *crema*—the froth that forms on top of the coffee—will be too thick and will add too much intensity. For Malabar, it is best to use a slow-extraction method, such as Chemex (2 ½ minutes extraction) or a French press (3 ½ minutes infusion).

3. The water temperature. In general, it should not rise above 194°F (90°C) so that the coffee is no hotter than 185°F (85°C); any hotter and its flavors will be affected.

How to best enjoy this pairing

For this pairing, the ideal temperature of the coffee is between 131 and 149°F (55–65°C). This brings the temperatures of the two elements of the pairing closer together.

The Camembert is best enjoyed at room temperature to bring out all its flavors. So, take it out of the fridge at least an hour before you want to eat it.

I recommend that you drink the coffee from a wine glass. This will allow you to admire its thick, cloudy, and syrupy appearance. The fine rim will give you a better perception of the experience.

Finally, to taste, I recommend that you eat a mouthful of Camembert then take a sip of the coffee. You can accompany it with an oat or whole wheat cracker, which will add a crunch in your mouth and bring out the melting texture of the Camembert and the silkiness of the coffee. The naturally mild taste of the coffee will coat the palate and combine perfectly with the flavor of the Camembert.

What time of day?

Not for breakfast, that is for sure. Few people will appreciate woody and earthy notes in the morning. Most people will also want to avoid coffee at dinnertime, not least because Malabar contains quite a heavy dose of caffeine. I would recommend this pairing to end a lunch on a gourmet and pleasant note.

MISO WITH TAHINI

By **Philippe Bachmann**, chef and teacher at the Institut Paul Bocuse.

I chose to present this pairing because I have a particular fondness for miso. I lived in Asia for a long time, where miso is a staple ingredient. There, I tasted this pairing accompanied with tofu threaded onto skewers, like yakitori. It was truly amazing.

MISO

Miso is quite a thick paste made from rice and fermented soybeans. In Japan, where it has been used since immemorial, it is often served with sake and an egg yolk. It is very salty and is generally considered to have a umami flavor. A key ingredient in Asian cuisine, it is also present in fermented fish and tofu. It is this umami flavor that gives it its character and depth. For this recipe, I chose a fairly pale miso paste as it has a subtle taste that will not unsettle those unfamiliar with it. If you are familiar with its very particular taste, you can use a darker miso.

The fermentation of miso

Three ingredients are required to make miso: koji (a fine mold produced by the fermentation of rice), soybeans, and salt. Koji serves to ferment the soybean puree, a process that takes between three and six months in a cool, dry place. It is during this period that it will acquire all its flavors. The longer the fermentation period, the more ocher/dark brown in color the miso will be. Conversely, miso that has been fermented for only a short time will be white.

SESAME PASTE OR TAHINI

Tahini—sesame paste—is an Asian product. Very fatty and thick, it is made by crushing roasted sesame seeds. It has walnut and hazelnut flavors with lightly salty mineral notes.

Why does it work?

The blend of these two pastes creates a creamy and fairly rich marinade. The fattiness brings out the flavors and gives the recipe depth. Miso is a very salty and tart product (especially when aged). Tahini, which has a nutty, roasted taste with a hint of beans, adds some sweetness to the mixture. The sugar tones down the saltiness of the miso even more. The lemon juice enlivens the sauce and helps bind it by cutting through the fattiness of the sesame seeds. The recipe I am presenting here is inspired by hummus. The latter is made from sesame seeds and chickpeas with a little lemon juice. Here, the chickpeas are replaced with soybeans/miso. With its fairly neutral and mild taste, eggplant counterbalances the very strong flavors of the miso and sesame.

GRILLED EGGPLANT WITH WHITE MISO,
TAHINI, AND FRESH QUINOA

Serves 4

- 2 eggplants
- 3 tbsp olive oil
- 1 oz. (25 g) white miso
- 1 tsp tamari (the liquid from the manufacture of miso)
- 2 tsp (⅓ oz./10 g) grated fresh ginger
- 1 tbsp rice vinegar
- 2 tsp (⅓ oz./10 g) tahini
- 1 tsp sugar
- 1 cup + 1 tbsp (3 ½ oz./100 g) quinoa
- 1 tbsp lime juice
- 1 cucumber, sliced
- 2 scallions, sliced
- 8 basil leaves
- Salt

HOTEL MANAGER BERNARD RICOLLEAU'S RECOMMENDED PAIRING:

Ikebana beer, English IPA, Ouroboros brewery (France). To marry the different textures of this dish, opt for complementarity with this lively beer with floral notes, which will bring out the flavors of the eggplant, and freshness, which will tone down the tahini.

Philippe BACHMANN's recipe

1. Preheat the oven to 340°F (170°C/Gas mark 3).

2. Wash the eggplants, cut them in half lengthwise, and score the flesh with a knife. Brush with olive oil, sprinkle lightly with salt, and roast in the oven for 20 minutes.

3. Blend the miso with the tamari, ginger, vinegar, tahini, and sugar. Spread this mixture over the cut surface of the eggplant (reserving some for dressing the salad) and place in the oven until the top is golden.

4. Meanwhile, rinse the quinoa in a fine-mesh sieve, then tip it into a saucepan and add one and a half times the volume of water. Bring to a boil and cook for 10 minutes. Remove the saucepan from the heat, let the quinoa plump for 5 minutes, then drain.

5. Tip the quinoa into a dish and stir in the lime juice, cucumber, scallions, and basil leaves (cut into strips or left whole).

6. Season with the reserved miso glaze. Arrange on the plates.

You could accompany this dish with traditional Chinese *mantou* bread, which is made with rice flour and steam cooked.

What if there is miso left over?

As miso paste is very salty, only a small quantity is needed to flavor a whole dish. If, having made your dish, you have some left over, you can use it to ferment vegetables, as with classic lacto-fermentation (see p. 46). Simply replace the salt with the miso and let your vegetables ferment open to the air for twenty-four hours, then place them in the fridge to stop fermentation. You can also marinate meat or fish using this method. In this case, fermentation will occur in the fridge. Miso paste will give your vegetables a very pleasant umami flavor.

SAUERKRAUT WITH PIGEON, JUNIPER, FOIE GRAS, AND SEA URCHIN

By **Marc Lahoreau**, Deputy Executive Chef at the Institut Paul Bocuse, sauce specialist.

I chose this recipe because it was one of the first ones I created for Yannick Alléno when I was working at the Royal Mansour in Morocco. I chose to pair it with sauerkraut because, for some time now, I have been getting very interested in fermentation.

SAUERKRAUT

For this pairing, I opted for raw fermented cabbage because it remains crunchy and adds some texture to the dish. This cabbage has an interesting tangy taste that gives my recipe a very pleasant depth. In addition, it balances out some of the fatty ingredients, such as the foie gras, for example. Good for your health, it activates digestion and adds a light touch. Here, I have decided to use it in two ways: fried in butter and raw.

PIGEON

This is a product typical of our region of Bresse, where pigeons are raised free range. I chose a young Bresse pigeon that had been fed by its parents on peas, beans, and corn for between twenty-eight and thirty-two days. Its flesh is fine and has a subtle taste.

Why does it work?

Roast pigeon is a classic French dish. By combining it with fermented cabbage, I have given it a new twist. This dish, both traditional and modern, relies on two basic principles: the contrasts and complementarity of the ingredients. Land and sea are represented by the pigeon and sea urchin and provide a clash of tastes and an explosion of flavors.
The canapés, topped with a pâté of chicken livers, foie gras, and sea-urchin corals, are balanced by the raw cabbage: the sourness offsets the fattiness. To accompany this dish, a crunchy sauerkraut, lightly fried in butter, is served on a bed of pilaf rice. The tanginess of the fermented cabbage enlivens the full-bodied and tasty jus. It adds vitality and enhances the aromatic notes. To connect these elements, I add juniper berries, which echo the flavors of the cabbage.
The tangy jus distilled from the fermented cabbage gives meaning to all these very distinct ingredients and really lifts the dish.

ROAST BRESSE PIGEON WITH JUNIPER BERRIES,

PILAF RICE, FERMENTED CABBAGE, AND TANGY JUS

Serves 4

For the roast pigeon
- 2 Bresse pigeons
- Scant ¼ cup (1 ¾ fl. oz./50 ml) olive oil
- ¼ cup (1 ¾ oz./50 g) butter

For the canapés
- 1 ½ tbsp (½ oz./15 g) finely chopped shallot
- Scant ¼ cup (1 ¾ fl. oz./50 ml) olive oil
- 3 ½ oz. (100 g) chicken livers
- 1 oz. (30 g) foie gras terrine
- ¾ oz. (20 g) sea urchin corals (about 6 large sea urchins)
- ¼ loaf of white sandwich bread
- ⅓ cup + 1 tbsp (3 ½ oz./100 g) clarified butter
- Salt and pepper

HOTEL MANAGER BERNARD RICOLLEAU'S RECOMMENDED PAIRING:

Mao Cha black tea from Yunnan, China. A black tea infused at room temperature. A "grand cru" with woody and vegetal notes that is slightly astringent to offset the acidity of the jus.

Marc LAHOREAU's recipe

1. Ask your butcher to cut up and then truss your pigeons so they keep their shape.

2. Sear them in the olive oil on all sides then roast in the oven with the butter until cooked to your liking, basting them occasionally.

3. Remove from the oven and let rest for the same amount of time as they were cooking. Reserve the cooking juices.

4. Remove the breast bones and lift the breast fillets.

5. Bone the thighs and trim the meat off the top of the thighs. Reserve the carcasses to use for the jus.

For the canapés

1. Sweat the shallot in the olive oil, then add the chicken livers to the pan and brown. Remove from the pan and let cool.

2. Pass the chicken livers, foie gras, and sea urchin coral through a fine sieve. Adjust the seasoning.

3. Refrigerate over ice.

4. Cut ½-inch (1-cm) thick slices of sandwich bread then cut into 2 ¾ × 2 ¾ × 1 ¼ inch (7 × 7 × 3 cm) triangles.

5. Fry the bread triangles in the clarified butter, drain on paper towel, then sprinkle with salt and pepper.

6. Spread the fried bread with the chicken liver, foie gras, and sea urchin coral mixture.

For the pilaf rice, fermented cabbage, and nori
- 1 cup (4 ½ oz./125 g) finely chopped white onion
- 2 ¾ tbsp (1 ¾ oz./50 g) butter
- 1 cup + 2 tbsp (7 oz./200 g) basmati rice
- 1 thyme sprig
- 1 ¼ cups (10 fl oz./300 ml) chicken stock
- ⅓ cup + 2 tbsp (3 ½ oz./100 g) butter
- 1 cup (5 oz./150 g) fermented cabbage
- 1 nori sheet

For the pigeon jus
- 2 pigeon carcasses, crushed
- Scant ¼ cup (1 ¾ fl. oz./50 ml) olive oil
- ⅓ cup + 2 tbsp (3 ½ oz./100 g) butter
- 1 thyme sprig
- 3 garlic cloves
- 2 juniper berries
- Sherry vinegar
- Scant ¼ cup (1 ¾ fl. oz./50 ml) fermented cabbage extract

To assemble and serve
- 2 tsp chopped chives
- 1 tsp fleur de sel
- 1 tsp coarsely ground white pepper
- 2 juniper berries, crushed
- ⅓ cup (1 ¾ oz./50 g) fermented cabbage
- A handful of nori

For the pilaf rice, fermented cabbage, and nori

1. Preheat the oven to 400°F (200°C/Gas mark 6). In a casserole with the lid on, sweat the onion in the 2 ¾ tbsp (1 ¾ oz./50 g) butter, then add the rice and cook until coated translucent. Add the thyme sprig and hot stock and cook, covered, in the oven for 18 minutes until all the stock has been absorbed.

2. Fluff up the rice using a fork and check the seasoning.

3. Melt the ⅓ cup + 2 tbsp (3 ½ oz./100 g) butter, add the fermented cabbage, and fry until colored. Remove from the heat, drain, and season with salt.

4. Set aside on paper towels.

5. Cut the nori sheet into thin strips 2 inches (5 cm) long.

For the pigeon jus

1. In a saucepan, brown the crushed pigeon carcasses in the olive oil, then add the butter, crushed garlic, and thyme and brown. Skim off the fat. Add the juniper berries, deglaze with the sherry vinegar, then add the reserved cooking juices.

2. Remove from the heat, strain, and reduce.

3. Check the seasoning and add the fermented cabbage extract.

To assemble and serve

1. Place the pigeon breasts, skin side up, and the lukewarm fermented cabbage on a plate and sprinkle with a mixture of chopped chives, fleur de sel, and freshly ground white pepper. Add the canapés and top with the crushed juniper berries.

2. Serve the hot rice, fried cabbage, and nori separately.

3. Serve the jus in a gravy boat.

CHOCOLATE WITH TARRAGON

By **Vincent Durant**, Meilleur Ouvrier de France, chocolatier and patisserie-chocolaterie teacher at the Institut Paul Bocuse.

Every day, I like to pair chocolate—my specialty—with ingredients that are available in my region of Ain. That's exactly what I wanted to do here. I created this recipe for the Meilleur Ouvrier de France contest, and it brought me luck: I won!

CHOCOLATE

For this pairing, I chose a Mexican chocolate that contains 66 percent cocoa solids. Mexico is the birth place of chocolate, which is why I am particularly attracted to this variety. The first impression you have is that it is very tart, but it soon releases woody and spicy notes with a touch of licorice. The finish is very fresh and really pleasant.

The fermentation of cocoa

After picking, the pods covering the cocoa beans, which are surrounded by a white pulp rich in water and sugar, are broken. The yeasts present on the outside of the pod then come into contact with the seeds and fermentation begins. The sugar is gradually changed into alcohol. Acetic bacteria present in the air then transform this alcohol into acetic acid. This is the moment the precursors of the aromas, which will be revealed when the cocoa beans are roasted, begin to emerge.

TARRAGON

Tarragon, which has large, long leaves, is best known for its role in sauces to accompany meat or fish and is a very commonly used herb in France. It has a spicy, woody, licorice taste.

Why does it work?

The aim of this recipe is to add a grassy, raw, natural, non-oxidized freshness, without betraying its natural aromas. In the mouth, sourness and the "bitter-fruity" notes of the chocolate contrast with the freshness of the tarragon. The strong taste of the tarragon balances that of the chocolate. For this pairing, I chose to make a ganache—a mix of cream and chocolate—which enables the delicate flavor of the tarragon to be revealed. It also adds a creaminess to the bitterness of the chocolate. On the finish, the freshness of the tarragon combines with the licorice note of the chocolate to create an ideal flavor with which to end a meal.

CHOCOLATE GANACHE WITH TARRAGON

Makes 40 chocolates
- ⅔ cup (6 fl. oz./170 ml) whipping cream
- ¾ oz. (22 g) tarragon leaves
- 2 ¼ tbsp (1 ¾ oz./50 g) glucose syrup
- 3 ½ oz. (100 g) dark chocolate, 66 percent cocoa solids
- 2 level tsp (⅓ oz./10 g) butter
- About 10 ½ oz. (300 g) dark couverture chocolate for the shells

HOTEL MANAGER BERNARD RICOLLEAU'S RECOMMENDED PAIRING:

Goat Me a Stout beer, Oatmeal Stout, La P'tite Maiz brewery (France).
A beer enriched with oats for a rich texture with coffee and bitter cacao flavors. Ideal with chocolate to finish a meal.

Vincent DURANT's recipe

1. Make the ganache. Boil the cream, then pour it over the tarragon leaves. Blend then strain.

2. Melt the 3 ½ oz. (100 g) dark chocolate. Heat this infusion with the glucose syrup to 104°F (40°C), then pour it over the melted chocolate.

3. Make the chocolate shells in molds, fill them with the ganache, then cover with a second layer of couverture chocolate.

You can accompany these chocolates with some malted bread, but make sure its taste is not so strong that it overpowers that of the tarragon.

FERMENTED SHRIMP CURRY PASTE WITH SCALLOPS

By **Florian Pansin**, chef at the Institut Paul Bocuse Saisons teaching restaurant.

I love this pairing because the ingredients bring out the best in each other. In it, you discover all the sensations that a dish can provide: sweetness with the scallops and coconut milk and zing with the ginger and lemon. The shrimp paste enhances all these flavors and makes this a real feast for the senses.

FERMENTED SHRIMP CURRY PASTE

Shrimp paste is a popular ingredient in Southeast Asia and Southern China which goes by different names in different countries. With an indefinable taste between tartness and bitterness, shrimp paste is difficult to eat on its own and its smell of aged dried fish is fairly unpleasant, too. But it acts as a flavor enhancer, intensifying the aromas of the spices it is mixed with. So, I decided to incorporate it in my curry paste. It is difficult to identify this ingredient when you taste this dish, but it gives it its depth.

The fermentation of shrimp paste

Shrimp paste is generally made from small shrimp that are rinsed, drained, then mixed with salt and left to rest for a day or two. They are then dried in the sun. During this fermentation period, the mixture will turn brown and will gradually transform into a dark pink or brown paste. Fermentation can last from a few days to a few months, depending on the size of the shrimp. Once the mixture is smooth, the paste is dried and cut into bricks.

SCALLOPS

I prefer semi-cooked scallops because they have more texture and have less of that sweet, sugary, vanilla-like taste. When you taste scallops cooked like this, you experience its two textures: smooth and creamy in the center and caramelized on the outside. It has a very fine, subtle flavor: sea-salty but with a hint of hazelnut.

Why does it work?

The shellfish taste of the fermented shrimp adds depth to the curry sauce and reveals the rather sweet taste of the scallops. The curry paste blends with the freshness of the lemon. In my recipe, there is also ginger to add a bit of spiciness, garlic to give depth, and lime, scallion, and tarragon for freshness. All the ingredients are important.

"DENTELLE" OF SCALLOPS
WITH LIGHTLY FERMENTED CURRY SAUCE

Serves 4

For the scallops
- 7 oz. (200 g) spinach
- 1 bunch scallions
- ½ bunch tarragon
- 1 ½ oz. (40 g) samphire greens
- 1 lime
- 2 tbsp (1 oz./30 g) butter
- 12 shelled scallops

For the dentelle
- 3 ½ tbsp (1 ¾ fl. oz./50 ml) water
- ¾ tbsp olive oil
- ¾ tbsp all-purpose flour

For the curry paste
- 1 shallot
- 1 bird's-eye chili (variable depending on how spicy you want it)
- ⅓ oz. (10 g) fresh turmeric
- 1 lemongrass stalk
- ⅓ oz. (10 g) fresh ginger
- 1 tbsp olive oil
- 1 tsp fermented shrimp paste
- 1 tbsp coconut milk

For the curry sauce
- Scant ½ cup (3 ½ fl. oz./100 ml) whipping cream
- 1 tbsp coconut milk
- 1 tbsp curry paste (see above)
- 1 lime
- Tabasco

HOTEL MANAGER BERNARD RICOLLEAU'S RECOMMENDED PAIRING:

Da Hong Pao semi-oxidized oolong tea, Fujian province, China.

Florian PANSIN's recipe

1. Wash the spinach and remove the stalks. In a pan of boiling salted water, cook the spinach leaves for 5 minutes. Rinse under cold water, then drain to remove as much water as possible.

2. Finely chop the green parts of the scallions and the tarragon.

3. Trim the samphire greens to leave only the thin tips.

4. Peel three strips of zest from the lime and cut into very fine strips. Remove the supremes and chop into small pieces.

5. Make the dentelle. In a mixing bowl, mix together all the ingredients using an immersion blender.

6. Make the curry paste. Peel and finely chop the shallot, chili, turmeric, lemongrass, and ginger.

7. Sweat all these ingredients in a pan in a drizzle of olive oil for a few minutes. Add the fermented shrimp paste and the coconut milk and simmer gently, covered, for about 20 minutes. Blend to a smooth paste.

8. Make the curry sauce. In a pan, heat the cream and coconut milk until simmering. Stir in 1 tablespoon of the curry paste, then season with the lime juice and Tabasco, adjusting the quantities depending on how sour and spicy you like it.

9. In a sauté pan, sauté the spinach in the butter.

10. Pour 1 spoonful of the dentelle mixture into a hot nonstick skillet, then place three scallops side by side on top. Cook gently, then remove carefully using a spatula.

11. Arrange the different vegetables on each plate. Drizzle some of the sauce around the outside.

You can accompany this dish with some curried cornbread.

BRIOCHE WITH FRAMBOISE BEER

By **Camille Dupuy**, Sensory Analysis Director at Lesaffre.

This pairing was born during a workshop organized for our employees and some of our customers. We had noticed that brioche and beer came from two very similar aromatic families. We therefore selected different combinations that we tasted with our visitors and it was this pairing that won all the votes.

FRAMBOISE (RASPBERRY) LAMBIC

This lambic is a rarity in the world of Belgian beers: only a few breweries offer a limited production during the summer. It has a magnificent ruby-red color and a fine and not very persistent head, typical of lambic. The nose reveals very fruity aromas of raspberry and, more generally, red berries. The mouth also evokes these fruity notes, but these are more balanced due to a slight tartness. The finish is both dry and fruity.

The fermentation of lambic
Lambic is a beer that has undergone spontaneous fermentation. Unlike other beers, the brewer adds no yeast to facilitate fermentation. The wort is exposed to the air so that yeasts present in the atmosphere infuse the beverage. This lambic serves as a base for all sorts of beers, including one flavored with raspberries (framboise), commonly known as *kriek*. During its manufacture, more than 10 ½ oz. (300 g) of fresh raspberries, as well as a small quantity of cherries, are added per liter of lambic. The beer is then aged in oak casks, which gives a marvelous result.

BRIOCHE

For this pairing, we chose a large brioche which is rich in butter—about 40 percent of the weight of flour. It is also quite sweet, containing about 20 percent sugar. It is vital that the butter be of high quality: a fine AOP butter, with its very pleasant taste, is perfect.
It is important that the brioche is well risen and that it has an open crumb. Ideally, it should contain a little yeast rich in lactic acid as this acts as a flavor enhancer and gives the aromas a long finish.

How to best enjoy this pairing
Begin the tasting by taking a sip of the beer and swirling it around in your mouth. Next, take a bite of the brioche, then, when you have swallowed it, take another sip of the beer.
Reheat the brioche. Heat concentrates the aromas. Before taking a bite, hold the brioche up to your nose: the smells of fermentation and butter will be even stronger.
Favor the center of the brioche. The fermented notes, which are the basis of this pairing, are very volatile, so they are more present in the center of the brioche as they are locked in there. The crust, with its caramel and toasted notes, has too strong a taste and will distort the balance of flavors.
Drink the beer from a flute. This type of glass is the best suited to allow you to sense all the aromas. Its thin glass and tall and narrow shape enable better preservation of the bubbles and flavors.

Why does it work?

This balance is based on the combination of aromas between the nose, the mouth, and the persistence of the taste. The first sip of beer will coat the tongue and palate. Almost metallic tasting, the lactic acid will open up the tastebuds everywhere in the mouth. After this first sip, the brioche will explode in the mouth like an acid drop. The lactic acid of the fermentation and the tart taste of the red berries complement each other; the red berry notes and the brioche almond notes enhance each other. These almond notes arise from the aromas of the butter mixed with the powerful fermentation aromas produced by the yeast.

The crumb should be light but consistent, so that the aromas are released fully as you chew. This lightness ensures that the brioche stays in your mouth for a shorter time and requires less chewing, thus contributing to the beer/brioche balance. The lactic acid contained in the yeast acts as a flavor enhancer and reinforces the tangy and subtle aromas of the red berries in the beer.

On the finish, the carbonic acid will cut through the fatty sensation left by the brioche and leave an impression of freshness.

The best time to enjoy this pairing

In the afternoon, this pairing makes for a delicious grown-up snack.

THE FUTURE OF FERMENTATION

In the pages of this book, we have explored the astonishing powers of fermentation, as well as those of yeasts and bacteria. Bread, wine, sauerkraut, and beer: the food we eat owes a great deal to fermentation.

But what of the future? In a world increasingly devoted to technology, will fermentation, a natural and traditional process, still have a place? Will it be able to adapt to new ways of eating and tomorrow's nutritional challenges?

TOMORROW'S NUTRITIONAL CHALLENGES

The way we eat has always been the product of our environment. Wars, developments in farming, and multiculturalism have, among many other factors, changed the way we eat. Today, in the West, we are giving greater importance to what we eat because we understand that food is key to staying healthy. The dishes we eat are more varied. We are favoring organic farming and buying local produce. We are consuming less meat—or avoiding it altogether. For some, eating has even become an act of protest.
In the near future, we will continue to face great challenges. By 2050, there will be nine billion people that will need to be fed without exhausting or further harming our planet's resources. Combined with the effects of global warming, this will require a complete change in the way we eat. In this context, how can we ensure the availability of the proteins that are so vital for our bodies? Fermentation is one of the keys to responding to this evolution, opening up a vast field of possibilities for preserving the planet and feeding its inhabitants.

YEASTS AND BACTERIA TO KEEP US HEALTHY

As we have seen, yeasts and bacteria are a natural part of our diet. In recent years, scientists have been studying their potential in the area of health. And there is no shortage of these microorganisms: in the form of nutritional supplements, they can have a positive effect on our brain function, digestive and reproductive systems, and joints, as well as on our general health. For example, the *boulardii* strain of *Saccharomyces cerevisiae*, the yeast that is used to made bread and wine, helps improve our intestinal microbiota—a real benefit for the digestive system.
Scientists use these yeasts and bacteria in the same way as in breadmaking. They first identify the microorganisms, selecting them for their specific abilities and different potentials. The aim is then to cultivate them in huge vats that enable them to reproduce, before drying and marketing them.
• The Earth contains an infinite number of microorganisms. The knowledge that has been acquired about fermentation enables scientists to make use of and develop them so that they can provide health benefits for humans and animals and also to manufacture specific compounds that will be extracted from the microorganisms.
There are limitless possibilities, provided that the

appropriate microorganism is identified and is placed in conditions where fermentation will allow it to develop its full potential. Some great surprises are in store for us.

• A process resulting from fermentation makes it possible to recover vitamins from certain yeasts via extraction. Once the yeasts have reproduced in huge vats, their molecules are broken down to extract the compound of interest.
S-adenosylmethionine (often called SAM-e) is a substance that occurs naturally in the human body and that we need in order to synthesize neurotransmitters such as serotonin and dopamine. If we lack them, we may experience mood swings or other emotional problems, which can also have a negative effect on our cellular and neurological health. This molecule also has beneficial effects on the health of the liver and joints. It is a metabolite of the amino acid methionine produced by living cells and helps maintain normal activity. A definite advantage is that this compound can be obtained by fermenting a *Saccharomyces cerevisiae* yeast, thereby compensating for deficiencies in the human body.

• Vitamin K2, which can also be obtained by fermentation, is very important for the body. It activates a group of proteins that helps bind calcium to our bones and prevent vascular calcification. It also has a beneficial effect on the cardiovascular system. The fermentation process makes it possible to obtain natural and pure K2 of optimal quality. Its use in food supplements means everyone can get access to it, just like in food (not necessarily fermented).

• Chondroitin (chondroitin sulfate) makes tendon and ligament cartilage stronger and more elastic. It is therefore particularly beneficial in cases of osteoarthritis or joint overload. Most often extracted from animal products—beef, pork, poultry, and some fish—chondroitin can now also be produced from fermented yeasts. This makes it possible to obtain an entirely plant-based product and to control the entire manufacturing process.

• Finally, to further intensify the benefits of yeasts, scientists have developed techniques to enrich them, with minerals, for example. There are two ways of doing this: either an individual yeast is fed so that it produces more of the element that is of interest, or this element is added after fermentation. This is notably the case for yeast enriched with selenium, which is involved in thyroid metabolism.
Research into biotechnology will develop further in the future. Microalgae, for example, which are very rich in proteins and vitamins, could provide numerous health benefits thanks to a fermentation process.

Eat more healthily with yeast extracts

Less fat, less salt, less sugar: we are constantly being reminded that our health depends at least in part on what we put on our plates. At the same time, public health decisions have been made and the food industry has had to adapt to new standards protecting consumer health.

Fermentation is a natural and healthy way to address these concerns. Yeast extracts enable manufacturers to reduce the fat, sugar, and salt content of their products without affecting their taste. As a result, we can eat food that is healthier without even being aware of the difference.

What is yeast extract?

Yeast extract is a natural ingredient derived from fresh yeast. The first step in its manufacture involves fermenting a specific type of yeast. As with breadmaking, this yeast will multiply on a very large scale. Then—and this is where yeast extract is different—scientists break down the cell to retrieve the compound they're interested in: yeast extract.
In the 1960s, yeast extract was promoted as a natural flavoring and the food industry listed it as a raw material for the manufacture of many foods. Today, yeast extract continues to be used for its multiple taste attributes in soups and stocks, sauces and cooking aids, snacks and seasonings, processed fish, meat and similar products, dairy products, sweet products, and starchy foods.

DID YOU KNOW ?

Did you know that certain micro-organisms are able to transform the ferulic acid from rice bran into natural vanillin by fermentation? Unlike natural vanilla extract, which is extracted straight from the pod, natural vanillin remains consistent over time, in terms of its quality, because it is not subject to the vagaries of weather conditions. In addition to its taste, which is much appreciated in pastries and ice creams, this totally natural flavor can also be used, in very small quantities, as a way to reduce the sugar content of brioches and intensify their buttery notes. In the future, this natural vanillin may give everyone access to this much sought-after flavor.

Healthier eating also means focusing on natural ingredients. Yeasts make it possible for manufacturers to both meet consumer expectations and comply with legislation. In fact, yeasts are totally natural, GMO-free, and thus constitute healthy and safe alternatives. They also all benefit from the "Clean Label," which guarantees they are natural.

Replacing meat or fish in a natural way

Today, 70 percent of the proteins in human food are of animal origin. Finding a substitute for meat or fish is therefore essential. The increase in world population is prompting research into alternative sources of protein that will be able to feed the whole world. The "meat analogue" or "fish analogue" trend is arousing growing interest throughout the world in all food sectors, from fast food to haute cuisine.

During the First World War, food shortages diminished supplies available for soldiers on the front. In Great Britain, Marmite®, a brown paste that smells of meat, tastes like meat, and contains many vitamins and proteins, was distributed to the soldiers. It was made from fermented yeast extracts. After the end of the war, Marmite® experienced significant growth and was even distributed in hospitals and canteens. Today, when saving the planet appears to be a very ambitious project given the growth in world population and the availability of food resources, the issue of meat consumption is becoming a social issue in many countries, not only for ecological reasons (livestock accounts for 14.5 percent of CO_2 emissions[53]), but also out of concern for animal welfare, for other ethical reasons, and for health reasons.

Here again, fermentation may provide an answer. In fact, it is now possible to manufacture a meat or fish substitute using this process. The principle remains the same: having selected certain yeasts, they are fed with carbohydrates, amino acids, and vitamins so that they produce the desired proteins. Specialists have managed to develop the flavors of salmon, chicken, and beef, for example, while ensuring the right nutritional intake of different types of meat.

Yeasts furthering the search for flavor

While it may be true that few chefs currently use yeast extracts in their cuisine, and it does not feature in their training, they are increasingly becoming interested in this trend. It is also a growing trend in home kitchens and it seems likely that its use will develop further. Used in cooking, yeast extract improves the taste of dishes and increases flavors dramatically—in the same way as do spices, fresh herbs, or leaving a dish to simmer for a long time. For example, it can give dishes a umami flavor. In the kitchen, yeast extract can add depth to a vegetarian dish or intensify the flavor of stocks.

The use of yeast extracts today mainly concerns the food industry, but it could soon open up a whole new realm for culinary experimentation for top chefs, who are constantly seeking creative ideas and ways to enhance flavors.

Fermentation is life

Fermentation has always been central to our diet. From the hanging of meat in prehistoric times to current research into biotechnologies, techniques may have evolved, but the principle remains the same: reliance on living organisms to improve human nutrition. Fermentation is life!

Notes

[1] Michel Perrin, *Le Chamanisme*. (Paris: Presses universitaires de France, 2014), 5–23.

[2] Claude Viel and Jean-Christophe Doré, "Histoire et emplois du miel, de l'hydromel et des produits de la ruche," *Revue d'histoire de la pharmacie*, no. 337 (2003): 14.

[3] Richard Evans Schultes and Albert Hofmann, *Les Plantes des dieux. Les plantes hallucinogènes, botanique et ethnologie*, (Paris: Berger-Levrault, 1981), 86.

[4] Éléonore Solé, "Découverte de la première brasserie 'industrielle' du monde," *Futura Sciences*, February 20, 2021, https://www.futura-sciences.com/sciences/actualites/archeologie-decouverte-premiere-brasserie-industrielle-monde-85794.

[5] Aude Le Floch, "L'Ayahuasca: usages traditionnels, pratiques modernes et perspectives thérapeutiques d'une boisson hallucinogène" (thesis supervised by Pierre-Nicolas Boivin, Université de Rennes, 2017), 50, https://ged.univ-rennes1.fr/nuxeo/site/esupversions/e5c21df7-0b24-4409-a37d-47841aa69e4c.

[6] Oswaldo Chinchilla Mazariegos, "Human sacrifice and divine nourishment in Mesoamerica: the iconography of cacao on the Pacific coast of Guatemala," *Ancient Mesoamerica* 27, no. 2 (2016): 361–75.

[7] Ecc. 31:27, AV.

[8] Gen. 9:20.

[9] Deut. 32:14.

[10] God called him "a high priest after the order of Melchizedek," Heb. 5:10.

[11] Gen. 14:18–19.

[12] Lionel Obadia, "Une ivresse rituelle? Ethnographie croisée de rites alcoolisés, entre chamanisme asiatique et judaïsme européen (Népal – France)," *Civilisations. Revue internationale d'anthropologie et de sciences humaines*, no. 66 (2017): 95–96.

[13] "And as they were eating, Jesus took bread, and blessed it, and brake it, and gave it to the disciples, and said, Take, eat; this is my body. And he took the cup, and gave thanks, and gave it to them, saying, Drink ye all of it; For this is the blood of the new testament, which is shed for many for the remission of sins. But I say unto you, I will not drink henceforth of this fruit of the vine, until that day when I drink it new with you in my Father's kingdom." Matt. 26:26–29.

[14] An image made popular by Saint Bonaventure, a thirteenth century Franciscan theologian. Like clusters of grapes in a winepress, his bodily members are wrung dry, blood flows, and the punishment incurred by humanity, which is mired in the poverty of sin, is removed.

[15] 2 John 1.

[16] "The kingdom of heaven is like unto leaven, which a woman took, and hid in three measures of meal, till the whole was leavened." Matt. 13:33.

[17] "And after this, Jesus knowing that all things were now accomplished, that the scripture might be fulfilled, saith, I thirst. Now there was set a vessel full of vinegar: and they filled a spunge [sic] with vinegar, and put it upon hyssop, and put it to his mouth. When Jesus therefore had received the vinegar, he said, It is finished: and he bowed his head, and gave up the ghost." John 19:28–30.

[18] Claude Arrieu, *Mouna, Mimouna, Achoura. Les fêtes de la convergence religieuse en Afrique du Nord avant 1962* (Aspet: PyréGraph, 2003).

[19] Massimo Montanari and Jean-Louis Flandrin, eds., *Histoire de l'alimentation* (Paris: Fayard, 1996), 36.

[20] Homer, *The Odyssey*, trans. A.T. Murray (Cambridge, MA.: Harvard University Press, 1919).

[21] Jared Diamond, *Guns, Germs, and Steel: The Fates of Human Societies* (New York: Norton, 2005).

[22] Marie-Claire Frédéric, *Ni cru ni cuit. Histoire et civilisation de l'aliment fermenté* (Paris: Alma Éditeur, 2014), 40.

[23] Marie-Claire Frédéric, "Un poisson fermenté de dix mille ans!", *Ni cru, ni cuit. Le blog des aliments fermentés*, May 2, 2016, https://nicrunicuit.com/le-savez-vous/un-poisson-fermente-de-dix-mille-ans.

[24] Madeleine Ferrières, *Histoire des peurs alimentaires, du Moyen Âge à l'aube du XXe siècle* (Paris: Seuil, coll. Points Histoire, 2006), no. 359.

[25] Ibid., 275–79.

²⁶ Romain Malbranque, "La prévention du scorbut au cours des grandes expéditions maritimes du XVᵉ au XVIIIᵉ siècle" (pharmaceutical sciences thesis, Université de Rouen, 2014), 25.

²⁷ Patrick Berche, "L'histoire du scorbut," *Revue de biologie médicale*, no. 347 (March 2019): 52.

²⁸ Andrew Curry, "Archaeology: The Milk Revolution," *Nature,* no. 500 (August 1, 2013), 20–22.

²⁹ Sarah B. McClure, Clayton Magill, Emil Podrug, et al., "Fatty acid specific δ¹³C values reveal earliest Mediterranean cheese production 7,200 years ago," *PLOS ONE* (September 5, 2018), https://doi.org/10.1371/journal.pone.0202807.

³⁰ Jared Diamond, *Collapse: How Societies Choose to Fail or Succeed* (London: Penguin Books, 2005), 224.

³¹ Ibid.

³² Frédéric, *Ni cru, ni cuit*, 122.

³³ Alain Schifres, *Dictionnaire amoureux du bonheur* (Paris: Plon, 2011).

³⁴ Jean-Pierre Brun, "La viticulture en Gaule : *Testimonia*," *Gallia*, no. 58 (2001): 236.

³⁵ Montanari and Flandrin, *Histoire de l'alimentation*, 64–65.

³⁶ Ibid., 212.

³⁷ Nathan Myhrvold and Francisco Migoya, *Modernist Bread* (Bellevue: The Cooking Lab, vol. 1, 2017), 34–37.

³⁸ Ferrières, *Histoire des peurs alimentaires*, 155.

³⁹ Steven L. Kaplan, *The Bakers of Paris and the Bread Question, 1700–1775* (London: Duke University Press, 1996), 37.

⁴⁰ J. W. von Goethe, *Campaign in France in the Year 1792*, trans. Robert Farie (London: Chapman and Hall, 1849), 103.

⁴¹ Paul Bocuse, "De la gastronomie française comme point d'ancrage des relations internationales," *Géoéconomie* 78, no. 1 (2016): 139.

⁴² Paul Grimal and Théodore Monod, "Sur la véritable nature du 'garum'," *Revue des études anciennes* 54, no. 1–2 (1952): 31.

⁴³ "At the present day, however, the most esteemed kind of garum is that prepared from the scomber, in the fisheries of Carthago Spartaria: it is known as 'garumn of the allies,' and for a couple of congii we have to pay but little less than one thousand sesterces. Indeed, there is no liquid hardly, with the exception of the unguents, that has sold at higher prices of late." Pliny the Elder, *The Natural History*, trans. John Bostock, Book 31, Chapter 43 (London: Taylor and Francis, 1855).

⁴⁴ Grimal and Monod, "Nature du 'garum'," 36.

⁴⁵ Andrew Smith, "From Garum to Ketchup. A Spicy Tale of Two Fish Sauces," in *Fish, Food from the Waters*, ed. Harlan Walker (Totnes: Prospect Books, 1998), 299–306.

⁴⁶ Antoine Lavoisier, *Traité élémentaire de chimie* (Paris, 1864 [1789]), 101–2.

⁴⁷ Marc V. Catsaras, "Louis Pasteur à Lille et les fermentations," *Bulletin de l'Académie vétérinaire de France*, no. 68 (1995): 421–22.

⁴⁸ When Pasteur filed his patent on June 26, 1871, he wrote, "I want the beers produced using my method to bear the name *Bière de la Revanche Nationale* (beer of national revenge)." In Jean-Claude Bologne, *Histoire morale et culturelle de nos boissons* (Paris: Robert Laffont, 1991).

⁴⁹ Fabrice Rousselot, "*Penicillium camemberti* : et l'homme créa le camembert," *The Conversation* (October 21, 2020), https://theconversation.com/penicillium-camemberti-et-lhomme-crea-le-camembert-147116.

⁵⁰ Guy Debord, "Abat-faim," *Encyclopédie des nuisances* (November 1985), pamphlet. 5, 102.

⁵¹ https://www.spiritueux.fr/spiritueux/eaux-de-vie-de-fruits

⁵² To find out more, watch her TED talk, "Grow Your Own Clothes," March 2011. TED Video, 6:24. https://www.ted.com/talks/suzanne_lee_grow_your_own_clothes?

⁵³ P. J. Gerber, H. Steinfeld, B. Henderson, A. Mottet, C. Opio, J. Dijkman, A. Falcucci, and G. Tempio, *Tackling climate change through livestock – A global assessment of emissions and mitigation opportunities* (Rome: FAO, 2013).

ACKNOWLEDGMENTS

Flammarion would like to thank Lesaffre for the chance to participate in a wonderful editorial adventure, in which we have discovered microorganisms (yeasts and bacteria) for breadmaking, taste, nutritional health, and biotechnology. In particular, we wish to thank Stéphan Béague for his supervision and support throughout the creation of this book. His valuable advice has enabled us to present the secret world of these infinitely tiny microorganisms to a wide readership.

This book would not have been complete without the expertise of Philippe Caillat, Cécile Chevreux, Marion Charzat, Camille Dupuy, Géraldine Esparceil, Jeanne Gallerand, Stéphane Pucel, Stéphane Lacroix, and Nicolas Zabukovec. We thank them for sharing their enthusiasm, expertise, and knowledge with us.

The publisher would also like to sincerely thank Stéphane Ros, who has put his passion and expertise into this book, as well as Sixtine Ros, Gilles Piat, and Nicolas Villion, whose talents and creativity have enabled us to beautifully illustrate the work.

The book would not exist in this form without the expertise of the Institut Paul Bocuse, its team of chefs, Agnès Giboreau, and Estelle Petit, who helped us decipher the alchemy of fine food and promote pairings of fermented dishes.

Finally, we would like to thank Marie-Laure Fréchet, who has kindly allowed us to use some of the recipes from her book *Upper Crust: Homemade Bread the French Way* (Flammarion, 2021), and the restaurant La Maniguette, which supplied us with several of their fermented specialties (salmon gravlax, duck brest, pickles, etc.), which enabled us to make photographs for this book.